Book 2

Just Vocabulary

Pre-Intermediate

Includes Answer Key

Jeremy Harmer
Ana Acevedo
Carol Lethaby
with Cheryl Pelteret

Viva Books
New Delhi | Mumbai | Chennai | Kolkata | Bangalore | Hyderabad | Kochi | Guwahati

First Indian Edition 2009

VIVA BOOKS PRIVATE LIMITED

- 4737/23 Ansari Road, Daryaganj, New Delhi 110 002
  E-mail: vivadelhi@vivagroupindia.net, Tel. 42242200
- 76, Service Industries, Shirvane, Sector 1, Nerul, Navi Mumbai 400 706
  E-mail: vivamumbai@vivagroupindia.net, Tel. 27721273, 27721274
- Jamals Fazal Chambers, 26 Greams Road, Chennai 600 006
  E-mail: vivachennai@vivagroupindia.net, Tel. 28290304, 28294241
- B-103, Jindal Towers, 21/1A/3 Darga Road, Kolkata 700 017
  E-mail: vivakolkata@vivagroupindia.net, Tel. 22836381, 22816713
- 7, Sovereign Park Apartments, 56-58, K. R. Road, Basavanagudi, Bangalore 560 004
  E-mail: vivabangalore@vivagroupindia.net, Tel. 26607409, 26607410
- 101-102 Mughal Marc Apartments, 3-4-637 to 641, Narayanguda, Hyderabad 500 029
  E-mail: vivahyderabad@vivagroupindia.net, Tel. 27564481, 27564482
- First Floor, Beevi Towers, SRM Road, Kaloor, Kochi 682 018, Kerala
  E-mail: vivakochi@vivagroupindia.net, Tel: 0484-2403055, 2403056
- H. No. 12, P. B. Road, Near Arya Hospital, Rehabari, Guwahati 781 008
  E-mail: vivaguwahati@vivagroupindia.net, Tel: 0361-2735624

www.vivagroupindia.com

Published by arrangement with

Marshall Cavendish Education
119 Wardour Street
London W1F 0OW, UK

ISBN-10: 81-309-1106-X
ISBN-13: 978-81-309-1106-9

Published by Vinod Vasishtha for Viva Books Private Limited, 4737/23, Ansari Road, Daryaganj, New Delhi - 110 002. Printed and bound by Raj Press, R-3, Inderpuri, New Delhi - 110 012.

Contents

Introduction

For the student

Welcome to *Just Vocabulary*. You can use this book with other students and a teacher, or you can work alone with it.

In this book you will find 16 units. Each unit has a section on useful vocabulary (with pictures, texts and explanations). There is then a section on language 'functions' (that means conversational English for use in many different situations). In the 'functions' sections you will learn how to say things.

There is an accompanying CD to help you with the many dialogues and pronunciation exercises in the book. Where you see the symbol ( ) it means that you can listen to the CD. You will also find an Audioscript at the back of the book which contains all the language on the CD.

When you see this symbol ( ) it means that the answers to the practice exercises are in the Answer key at the back of the book. You can check your answers there.

We hope that this book helps you progress in English, and, above all, that you enjoy using it.

For the teacher

This book is part of a series designed to be used alone or to supplement any course book you may be using. Each book in the series specialises in either language skills or aspects of the English language. It can be used either in class or by students working on their own.

Just Vocabulary consists of 16 units. Each unit is divided into two sections. In the first section, vocabulary for a variety of topic areas is introduced and practised. Topics include jobs and work, public transport, and giving and receiving. There are also units on two-word nouns and phrasal verbs, etc. The second section concentrates on functional areas such as expressing preference, asking for and giving advice, and apologising.

All the dialogue and pronunciation material has been recorded onto the CD, and there is an Audioscript at the back of the book.

Students will be able to use the book without needing explanation or guidance on the part of the teacher, and they can check their work in the comprehensive Answer key at the back of the book. However, the units are also highly appropriate for work in class.

We hope you find this book a real asset and that you will also try the other books in the series: *Just Reading and Writing*, *Just Grammar* and *Just Listening and Speaking*.

UNIT 1

A Vocabulary

Two-word nouns

1 Make two-word nouns. Join a word in column A with a word in column B.

A	B
car	~~office~~
cash	station
police	centre
travel	agent
petrol	stop
~~post~~	hire
shopping	dispenser
bus	station

a post office

b ....

c ....

d ....

e ....

f ....

g ....

h ....

2 Join the words in the boxes to make two-word nouns. Use the new nouns to label the pictures *a–h*.

cricket	match
car	station
~~phone~~	~~box~~
road	park
tea	bag
traffic	signs
underground	lights
letter	box

a phone box

b ....

c ....

d ....

e ....

f ....

g ....

h ....

3 Make two-word nouns for the following items using words from the descriptions.

a a book with useful phrases in a foreign language ......a phrase book......
b a room in a hotel ....
c a hat to keep off the sun ....
d glasses to protect you from the sun ....
e a calculator that you can put in your pocket ....
f a bag for sleeping in ....
g a book to guide you on your trip ....
h a camera to make a video ....

4 Write two-word nouns for the definitions.

a a shop where you can buy books ....a book shop....
b a sandwich made with chicken ....
c a shop where you can buy music ....
d a cake made with fruit ....
e a biscuit made with chocolate ....
f a cup for drinking tea ....
g a chair with arms ....
h a paper that contains news ....
i a place where cars park ....
j a ticket for a concert ....

5 Make as many new two-word nouns from the following words as you can. Check your answers in a dictionary.

book ....
card ....
football ....
hand ....
light ....
music ....

WORD BANK

Practise your new words.

a Write new words from this unit on small cards.
b Draw a picture and write a definition or a translation on the other side of the card.
c Put the cards in a box or a bag and mix them up.
d Take them out one at a time. Be careful to only look at one side. If it is the picture, say the English word. If it is the English word, translate it into your language.
e Check if you were right by turning the card over.

B Functions
Expressing preferences

A

B

1 Look at the photos. Which place …

a is more interesting to visit? ....

b is more relaxing? ....

c is more fun? ....

2 Read Fran and Sonia's comments. Choose the best holiday for them. Write Picture A or B.

Make a note of the reasons for your choice.

FRAN: I love watersports and sunbathing. I like sunny weather, ice cream and the smell of sun tan lotion. I don't want to do anything when I'm on holiday, except lie in the sun and relax.

Picture .... , because ....

....

....

SONIA: I like sunshine, but I get bored easily. I need lots of interesting things to do, like sightseeing or learning about different cultures. I'm interested in history, different languages and exploring new places.

Picture .... , because ....

....

....

....

....

3 Complete the dialogue with adjectives from the box. Use the correct form.

cheap
interesting
sunny
~~relaxing~~

SONIA: So which is better, then, Fran? Marbella or Dublin?

FRAN: Marbella, definitely. It's more (**a**) ...relaxing... , and it's (**b**) .... ! And it's got lovely beaches.

SONIA: But we always go to the beach. I'd rather do something different this year. Something more (**c**) .... Like a city. Like Dublin.

FRAN: There's a problem, then, Sonia.

SONIA: Oh? What's that?

FRAN: Because I like beaches. Well, I like beaches better than cities, anyway. And Marbella is (**d**) .... too. And it always rains in Ireland, you know, Sonia.

SONIA: No, it doesn't. And anyway, rain or no rain, there's more to do in Dublin.

FRAN: Like what? Museums and things like that? I'd rather stay here in London!

SONIA: OK then. You go to the beach and I'll go to Dublin. How's that?

FRAN: Oh, all right. You win. This time. But no museums, and no walking around in the rain!

4 Now listen to Track 1 and check your answers.

a What's the final decision? ....

b What expression does Fran use to accept Sonia's decision? ....

5 Complete the table with phrases from the dialogue in exercise 3.

Asking about preferences	Expressing preferences
Which would you rather do?	I prefer cities to beaches.

6 Complete the dialogue with expressions from the box. Then listen to Track 2 and check your answers.

I'd rather
~~Which do you prefer?~~
I prefer
Would you rather

SAM: Which package is better, then?

JACK: Oh, Package 3, definitely. It's cheaper! (a) Which do you pefer?

SAM: Me? I prefer package 1. It sounds much nicer.

JACK: But it's more expensive and shorter. Anyway, (b) .... summer holidays to winter holidays.

SAM: But the summer is nice here too. (c) .... go in December, when it's dark and cold here.

JACK: OK, you win. But that's the only holiday we can take in the whole year then. (d) .... have just one holiday, or two? Think about it.

SAM: Oh. Maybe July is not so bad after all …

7 Write the dialogue. Use suitable expressions from the box in exercise 6.

A: You want to go out tonight. Ask B for an opinion, the cinema or a restaurant?

....

B: Tell A that your choice is to go to the cinema.

....

A: Try to find out which type of film B wants to see – a comedy or a drama?

....

B: Tell A your personal choice is to see a comedy.

....

A: OK, you win! Let's find out what comedies are showing at the moment.

UNIT 2

A Vocabulary

Uncountable noun phrases

1 **Make phrases using the uncountable nouns from the box with the amounts and containers in the pictures. Some of the nouns can be used with more than one amount or container.**

bread	cake	cereal	cheese
lemon juice	milk	oil	salt
soup	sugar	water	

a (a bowl) a bowl of soup, a bowl of milk, a bowl of sugar

b (a slice) ....

c (a cup) ....

d (a drop) ....

e (a jug) ....

f (a pinch) ....

g (a spoonful) ....

h (a glass) ....

2 **Guess the mystery word. We can use the same word with all the following uncountable nouns in the phrase 'a .... of ....'. Use the clues to try to guess the word.**

furniture	homework	advice
information	clothing	news

Clues

a You use this word to talk about a quantity of bread. (Can't guess? Try the next clue.)

b You also use this word to talk about a sheet of paper.

c You also use this word to talk about a portion of cake.

d Still can't guess? Unscramble the letters: EECPI.

3 **Copy and complete the sentences. Use the mystery word and the nouns in exercise 2.**

a How many .... of .... did you do for English last week?

b You won a prize? That's a great .... of .... !

c That table is a lovely .... of ....

d You feel stressed? Let me give you a .... of .... : relax a bit.

e The report is almost finished. We just need one more .... of ....

f A shirt is a .... of .... , usually for men.

4 Label the picture with phrases 'a ...... of ......'. Choose words from the table. You will need to use some of the words twice; some are not used at all.

a a bowl of soup
b ....
c ....
d ....
e ....
f ....
g ....

			bread
	bowl		cake
	jug		coffee
	cup		cream
	drop		ice cream
a	glass	of	lemon juice
	tablespoon		orange juice
	slice		rice
	pinch		salt
			soup
			tea
			water

5 Add more nouns to the right-hand column of the table, such as salad, meat, etc. Use your words to make up two lunch 'menus' and write them in your notebook.

Example: *a bowl of salad, a cup of hot chocolate with a tablespoon of cream, ...*

WORD BANK

Make a special Word Bank notebook.

a Write new phrases from this section. Draw a picture, or write a translation for each word.

b Revise your words every now and then; look at the words and their meaning and say the phrases aloud.

c Choose some of the words and phrases in this section. Put them on cards and add them to your bag or box (see Word Bank, Unit 1).

B Functions

Asking for and giving advice

1 Listen to Track 3 and put the pictures in the right order.

a, ...

2 Complete the dialogue with suitable words. (You can use the words more than once.)

LISA: What's up, Maggie?
MAGGIE: Uh? Oh, I need to relax. Got any ideas?
LISA: Yes. Try exercise. Go to a (**a**) .... or something.
MAGGIE: No thanks. I don't like exercise.
LISA: OK, then. How about aromatherapy?
MAGGIE: What's that exactly?
LISA: It's a mixture of (**b**) .... and smells and (**c**) .... Very, very relaxing.
MAGGIE: Massage? That's not for me, I'm afraid.
LISA: You ARE difficult, Maggie.
MAGGIE: Sorry!
LISA: I know. You can close your (**d**) .... and count (**e**) .... Slowly.
MAGGIE: How many (**f**) .... ?
LISA: You could count up to, say, 33,781.
MAGGIE: 33,7...... .
LISA: Maggie? Maggie ... ha, ha.

Listen to Track 3 again and check your answers.

3 Listen to Track 3 again. Cover the dialogue in exercise 2. Tick the phrases in the box that you hear.

Asking for advice	Giving advice
Can you give me some advice?	Try ......
Got any ideas? ✓	How about ...... ?
What can I do ......?	You can ......
	You could ......

4 Give Maggie advice about how to relax. Use the prompts in brackets.

a have a cup of warm milk before bed (try)
Try having a cup of warm milk before bed.

b do not eat too much at night (how about)
....

c do not watch television in bed (try)
....

d listen to some relaxing music (you could)
....

e have a long warm bath (how about)
....

f go for a short walk (you can)
....

5 Read Leyla's problem on the right.

> I have exams next week and I don't know anything! What can I do to pass?

Complete Rob's advice. Use the expressions in the box in exercise 3.

a ......Try...... studying your notes.
b You .... do some of the practice questions, too.
c You .... do some of the exercises in the book.

6 Now use the other expressions in the box to make sentences giving advice to Leyla.

ROB: Hi, Leyla! You don't look too happy. Problems?
LEYLA: I have exams next week and I don't know anything! (a) ......What can I do...... to pass?
ROB: Hey, relax! (b) .... studying your notes.
LEYLA: Yeah, I looked at them, but it doesn't help.
ROB: Well, of course, just looking doesn't help. You (c) .... some of the practice questions, too.
LEYLA: Hmm, yes. But what about maths? I don't understand anything! (d) .... ideas?
ROB: Well, you (e) .... do some of the exercises in the book. Don't worry! That's my advice!
LEYLA: You're right. Let's forget about exams. Do you want to listen to my new J-Lo record?

Listen to Track 4 and check your answers.

7 You are Rob. Listen to Track 4 and read out Rob's words after the beep.

8 Give advice for these situations. Use the expressions in the box in exercise 3.

> I need to lose some weight!

Go to the gym.
Eat less.
Give up sweets and fatty food.
Take up running.

> I get very nervous before an exam.

Take a deep breath.
Close your eyes and imagine something pleasant.
Relax your shoulders.

UNIT 3

A Vocabulary

Reading, watching, listening

1 **Write the words from the box in *a*, *b* or *c*. You can use the words more than once.**

~~a comic~~ a magazine a newspaper a programme the news an article a report the weather forecast

a You read a comic, ...

b You watch ....

c You listen to ....

2 **Match the definitions *a–h* with the shows. Write the letters in the boxes.**

documentary ☐

soap opera ☐

cartoon ☐

game show ☐

news ☐

reality show ☐

sitcom ☐

talk show ☐

a A radio or television story about the lives of a group of people. It's on almost every day and doesn't have an end. It's usually very dramatic/exciting.

b A radio or television programme that gives people information, every day, about things that are happening in the world.

c A competition on radio or television – people win prizes.

d A programme with real people, not actors.

e A programme with facts and information about nature, historical events or science.

f A presenter invites famous people to the studio and they talk about different things.

g A funny story each week about the same group of people. They are usually in the same place.

h Adventures and funny stories, made with drawings and pictures – not real people and scenery.

3 **Complete the table with words from the box. You can use the words more than once.**

programme station channel article presenter ~~headline~~ journalist reporter news reader disc jockey (DJ)

The media	Related words
Radio	
Television	
Newspapers and magazines	headline

4 **Read the situations. Write sentences to tell the people what to do, as in the example. Use these verbs and phrases.**

read watch listen to	a comic a magazine a newspaper a programme the news an article a film the radio television the weather forecast

a JAKE: I want to know what is new in the world. What can I do?

YOU: Well, you could read a newspaper, or listen to the news.

b CAROLINE: What can I do to find out about the new fashions?

YOU: ……………………………………

c YOUR EIGHT-YEAR-OLD NEIGHBOUR: I'm bored! Got any ideas?

YOU: ……………………………………

d CINDY: This flight is so long!

YOU: ……………………………………

e ANYA: Shall I take an umbrella? Is it going to rain?

YOU: ……………………………………

f JOE: I have a cold. I have to stay in bed all day! What can I do?

YOU: ……………………………………

g PAM: I've finished my book and I'm still waiting to see the dentist! What can I do now?

YOU: ……………………………………

WORD BANK

Using new words in sentences helps you to remember them better. Write sentences with these words.

documentary
soap opera
sitcom
cartoon
game show
talk show
reality show

Example: My favourite sitcom is Friends.

……………………………………

……………………………………

……………………………………

……………………………………

……………………………………

……………………………………

……………………………………

B Functions

Discussing opinions

1 Look at the picture. Can you guess what the people are talking about?

Now listen to Track 5. Were you right?

2 Who says these things, *Jane* or *Lisa*? Write *J* or *L*.

a ☐ What do you think of soaps now? ....

b ☐ I hate soaps. They're silly stories. ....

c ☐ No, they're not. Oh, shhhhh. It's about to start. ....

d ☐ Well, I don't agree. I think they're really exciting. ....

e ☐ What, now? I can't. *The Rich Cry Too* is about to begin. Don't you watch it? ....

f ☐ You're joking! Soap operas are for people who have nothing better to do. ....

g ☐ Actually, this is exciting! ....

h 1 Do you want to go out for a pizza? J

3 Put the dialogue in exercise 2 in the correct order. Number the boxes *1–8*.

Asking for an opinion:
Giving an opinion:
Agreeing: You're right. I agree.
Questioning opinions: Do you really think so?
Disagreeing:

4 Complete the table with the phrases in blue from exercise 2.

5 Listen to Track 6. Complete the list with the words you hear.

Words which mean 'really good': great, terrific,

....

....

Words which mean 'really bad': terrible,

....

....

6 **Match the beginnings of the sentences in column 1 with the correct groups of endings in column 2.**

Column 1	Column 2
a What do you think ...	1 documentaries about animals. / watching the news. / rap.
b Do you really ...	2 of documentaries? / of street surveys? / of Peter?
c I (don't) agree ...	3 so, too. / you're right. / they're interesting.
d I hate ...	4 with you. / that documentaries are boring. / with your ideas.
e I think ...	5 think so? / think soaps are stupid? / like watching TV?

a ....2....
b ....
c ....
d ....
e ....

7 **Complete the dialogue with questions or sentences from exercise 6. Then listen to Track 7 and check your answers.**

LOUISE: What (**a**) ....do you think of.... documentaries?

DAMIAN: I think they're boring.

LOUISE: Do you really (**b**) .... ?

DAMIAN: Yes, don't you?

LOUISE: No. (**c**) .... Well, sometimes.

DAMIAN: (**d**) .... Only sometimes. I hate (**e**) .... , for example.

LOUISE: Oops! I bought you a DVD about birds for your birthday.

DAMIAN: You're joking!

LOUISE: No. I really did.

DAMIAN: Oh, well, birds are fine. Birds are good. Actually, I love birds!

8 **Now write your own dialogue. Use the table in exercise 4 to help you.**

A: Find out what B's opinion is of reality TV shows.

....

....

B: You feel very strongly and negatively about reality TV shows. Tell A.

....

....

A: You're surprised to hear B's strong feelings. Question B's opinion.

....

....

B: Answer A's question, and find out if A agrees with you.

....

....

A: Tell B you don't agree. Say the shows you really hate are sitcoms.

....

....

B: Agree with A about sitcoms.

....

....

A Vocabulary

Jobs and work

1 Look at the dictionary entries. Then complete the sentences with *job* or *work*.

> **job *n.*** [C] **1** an activity you do to earn your living, especially if you are working for somebody else. *I have a job in a shop.*
> **2** a specific piece of work that has to be done. *Who does all the jobs around the house?*
> **work *n.*** [U] **1** an activity you are paid for doing, especially regularly. *What work do you do?* **2** a general word when you are talking about several different jobs. *He's got a lot of work to do.*

a ......Job...... is a noun that has a plural.
b I have a lot of .... to do at the office.
c Nat's .... is to wash cars.
d A roadie's .... sounds fun.
e I have several boring .... to do today, like cleaning my room.
f Mara is looking for a .... for the holidays.
g Are you looking for .... ? Look at the small ads in the paper.

2 Match the *work + preposition* phrases in the left-hand column with the phrases in the right-hand column.

a work in	1 a fast food restaurant
b work as	2 small children
c work for	3 a project
d work on	4 a computer programmer
e work out	5 a large company
f work with	6 the solution to a problem

a .... b .... c .... d .... e .... f ....

3 Complete the sentences with the phrases *a–f* in exercise 2. Use the correct verb form.

a Joe likes helping people. He ...works with... problem teenagers.
b I have to .... my presentation for tomorrow's class. It's still not very good.
c Do you still .... the same company?
d The teacher can't give us any help. We have to .... the answer for ourselves.
e Julie wants to .... a model.
f I hate .... this place!

4 Complete the sentences with *work* or *job*.

a What's your father's ....jab.......... ?

b Does he usually have a lot of .... ?

c I like doing projects, but they are hard ....

d Would you like to get a .... for the holidays?

e Charlie graduated from university last month. He needs to get a .... but he doesn't know what kind of .... he wants to do.

5 Complete the sentences with one of the prepositions in the box. Then unscramble the words in bold to find out the people's occupations.

as	for	in
on	out	with

a Peter works ....in.......... a club. His job is to throw out people who behave badly. Peter works as a **cernubo** ....bouncer.......... .

b Joni works .... a school. Her job is to teach English. She works .... children. At the moment she is working .... her students' marks. Joni works .... a **achteer** ....

c Lola works .... a radio station. Her job is to play music. At the moment she is working .... a project for a special show: she's working .... the money she needs. She works .... a **sidc yckoje** ....

d Ollie works .... a large company. He works .... animals. His job is to catch rats and other pests. Ollie works .... a **tscp nerctrollo** ....

e Rose works .... a famous band. She works .... sound equipment, like microphones. Her job is to check the equipment before a concert. She is working .... the preparations for a big concert. Rose works .... a **riedoa** ....

WORD BANK

Make a diagram like this in your Word Bank notebook. Write the words in exercise 5 in the right place. Can you add more words for each preposition?

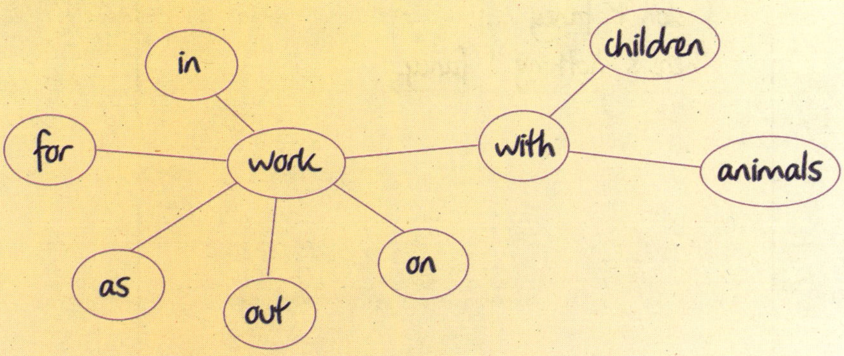

B Functions

Likes and dislikes

1 Listen to Track 8. Which advertisements are the people looking at? Tick the correct advertisements.

2 Listen to Track 8 again. Who says these things, Fred or Bella?

a Nah, there's nothing I fancy. ....
b I like children. ....
c I don't mind children. ....
d That's not for me. ....
e I'm not keen on animals. ....
f I love animals. ....
g I can't stand fast food places. ....
h It's not that bad. ....

3 Copy and complete the table with the phrases in exercise 2.

Ways to say you like something
I fancy …
Ways to say you don't like something (or it's not right for you)
I don't fancy … There's nothing I fancy.

Situations vacant

☐ **Wanted** A babysitter for 3 lovely children ages 6, 4 and 2. Evenings. Call 02028 657213

☐ **Making Waves** are looking for junior staff. This could be the beginning of a career in hairdressing. Call Jess on 082749

☑ **Calling animal lovers** The Animal Shelter is looking for people to help with unloved animals. Interested? Phone 04978826

☐ **Cool Gear** are looking for cool guys to work at our new branch. Good basic salary. Discount on all our clothes. Phone the manager on 095739 or 095720

☐ **Burger Lads** are hiring now for the holiday period. Good pay. Come and see us! 297 Main Street

☐ **Maths tutor** required. Are you good at Maths? Are you patient? Then you are the person we are looking for. Call Mrs Rock on 020 859 5637

4 **Put the verbs in the correct order from *a* (extreme dislike) to *e* (like very much).**

dislike	~~hate~~	like	love
not like			

a ....hate..........

b ....

c ....

d ....

e ....

5 **Complete the dialogue with the verbs and phrases in the box. Then listen to Track 9 and check your answers.**

love	~~(don't) like~~	fancy
keen on	can't stand	
don't mind	hate	

MAX: I am thinking of teaching after college. But I'm not sure.

MOLLY: Teaching? You? But you (**a**) ....don't like.... children.

MAX: I am not very (**b**) .... them. But I don't (**c**) .... them. Actually, I (**d**) .... really .... children – for a short time!

MOLLY: I (**e**) .... little children but I (**f**) .... big groups. I (**g**) .... a job teaching small groups.

MAX: Oh no, that's not for me. I want to get a temporary job to see if I like it.

MOLLY: That's a good idea.

6 **Write answers for the questions. Then listen to Track 10 and answer when it is your turn.**

Example:

INTERVIEWER: How do you feel about children?

YOU: ....I'm really keen on working with children....

a INTERVIEWER: How do you feel about children?

YOU: ....

b INTERVIEWER: Right. Now, tell me two things you like about teaching.

YOU: ....

c INTERVIEWER: And two things you definitely don't like?

YOU: ....

d INTERVIEWER: So, do you think teaching is right for you?

YOU: ....

UNIT 5

A Vocabulary

Public transport

1 Look at the pictures. Write the correct number in the boxes.

a Airport
Picture [4]

b Bus (coach) station
Picture [ ]

c Ferry terminal
Picture [ ]

d Railway (underground) station
Picture [ ]

bay barrier check-in desk
train escalator gate
passport control plane
platform lift
ticket machine ticket office

2 Complete the table with as many of the words from the box (under picture 4) in exercise 1 as possible. Some of the words can go in more than one column.

Airport	Coach (Bus) station	Ferry terminal	Railway/underground station
check-in desk			

3 Complete the announcements with the verbs in the box. Use some of them more than once.

a Passengers can ....board.... the plane at gate 34.
b .... the 36B bus to the city centre.
c .... the ferry 30 minutes before departure.
d .... to terminal 2 for flights to Asia.
e The flight .... at three thirty.

arrive board change
check-in go leave take

f .... the lift to the second floor.

g The train .... from platform 5.

h .... to gate 36.

i The train from Washington .... at five minutes past three.

j .... trains at Birmingham Central.

k You will have to .... planes at Dallas airport.

l .... 2 hours before your plane leaves.

4 **Match the words in the box and their meanings.**

board ~~escalator~~
gate lift airport
barrier platform
station ticket
terminal

a a moving staircase ....escalator....

b a place where you can get onto the train ....

c a piece of paper you need to travel on a train, plane or bus ....

d the place where you can take a plane ....

e a small room that carries people up and down ....

f the verb that means to 'get onto' a plane, train or bus ....

g the place where people wait before they get on the plane ....

h a thing that stops movement ....

i a place where you can take a ferry ....

j a place where you can get on a bus ....

5 **Complete this paragraph with the correct word.**

Lindy arrived at the (**a**) a i r p o r t and went immediately to the (**b**) c _ _ _ _ -i _ d _ _ _ and she showed her (**c**) t _ _ _ _ _ . She was flying to Brazil so she went up the (**d**) e _ _ _ _ _ _ _ _ to the international (**e**) t _ _ _ _ _ _ _ . It took her ten minutes to walk to her (**f**) g _ _ _ . She (**g**) b _ _ _ _ _ _ the plane.

At the end of the flight, when she (**h**) a _ _ _ _ _ _ in Brazil, she had to go through (**i**) p _ _ _ _ _ _ _ c _ _ _ _ _ _ _ . Then she picked up her (**j**) l _ _ _ _ _ _ and (**k**) t _ _ _ a (**l**) t _ _ _ to her hotel.

WORD BANK

Make a table like this in your Word Bank notebook. Put all the travel words you can find in this unit into the appropriate column. Some can go in more than one column. Add any other words you know that are not in the unit.

Plane	Train	Bus
ticket	ticket	ticket
airport	platform	

B Functions

Arranging to meet

1 Complete each gap in the dialogue with one word.

KIM: What time shall we meet, Max?

MAX: I could be (**a**) .... by about 11.

KIM: OK, (**b**) .... do you suggest?

MAX: Well, Kim, I could (**c**) .... at the top of the escalator, you know, (**d**) .... the entrance.

KIM: I've got a better idea. How (**e**) .... under the clock by platform 3?

MAX: OK. That sounds (**f**) .... Eleven o'clock it is then. (**g**) .... the clock.

KIM: Fine. See you (**h**) ....

Listen to Track 11. Did you have the same words as Kim and Max?

2 Complete the table with phrases *a–l*.

a Sounds great!

b Have you got any ideas/suggestions?

c How about the café on Logan Street?

d Let's meet under the clock.

e Let's say 8.30.

f OK, 8 o'clock it is, then.

g Or we could meet at the bus stop.

h That sounds good.

i We could meet at 8 o'clock.

j What's the best time to meet?

k Where do you suggest?

l Why don't we go to the Twenty-two Club?

Asking for suggestions	What time shall we meet?
Making suggestions	I could meet you at the top of the escalator.
Offering alternatives	I've got a better idea.
Agreeing	Fine. See you at 11.

3 Put these sentences in the right order to make a dialogue.

a JACKIE: Where's the best place to meet? [1]
b SANDY: See you there. [ ]
c JACKIE: Hmm. How about 7.30? [ ]
d JACKIE: Why don't we meet at Café Commons? [ ]
e JACKIE: OK. 7.30 it is, then. [ ]
f SANDY: OK. What time? [ ]
g SANDY: That sounds great. [ ]
h SANDY: Where do you suggest? [ ]

Now listen to Track 12 to check your answers.

4 Complete this dialogue.

YOU: (a) .... ?
MAYA: Let's say 6 o'clock.
YOU: (b) .... ?
MAYA: We could meet at the bus stop.
YOU: (c) .... ?
MAYA: OK. Good idea. We'll meet at the restaurant.
YOU: (d) ....
MAYA: See you there.

Now listen to Track 13 and respond when it's your turn.

UNIT 6

A Vocabulary

Life stages

adolescence (teens) adulthood ~~birth~~
childhood education marriage
parenthood romance work

1 Label the stages in Mark's life. Use words from the box.

a ......birth...... b .... c .... d ....

e .... f .... g ....

2 Write the words and phrases from the box on the lines.

to graduate from to fall in love
to get a job to have a baby
to get married to start school
to marry someone ~~to be born~~
to work as a ... to be dead
to die to be keen on someone

birth ......to be born......

education ....

work ....

romance ....

marriage ....

death ....

3 **Complete the passage with the correct form of the verbs in exercise 2.**

Mark was born in 1974. On 29th January, Mr and Mrs Thomas (**a**) ......had...... a baby. They called him Mark, after his father.

Little Mark (**b**) .... school when he was five years old.

When he was 16, Mark went out with Susan. He (**c**) .... on her but their romance did not last long and after school, he didn't see her again.

Mark (**d**) .... university in 1996 and soon (**e**) .... a job in a computer company, where he (**f**) .... a programmer.

At work, Mark met Susan again. This time they (**g**) .... for real.

Mark (**h**) .... his childhood sweetheart in 2001. They (**i**) .... on a balloon! It was a fantastic wedding and everyone had fun.

Mark's dad is now (**j**) .... He (**k**) .... a few years ago. Now Susan is expecting a baby. If it's a boy, she wants to call him Mark, after his dad and grandad.

4 **Read the passage in exercise 3 again. Find phrases related to:**

a birth ......was born on......

b education ....

c marriage ....

d work ....

e death ....

5 **Listen to Track 14. Answer the questions about yourself. Write full answers in the spaces.**

a ......My name's......

b ....

c ....

d ....

e ....

f ....

WORD BANK

Copy this table into your Word Bank notebook. Write the verbs and phrases in the box in the correct places in your table. Make sure you write the whole phrase.

life stages

birth	education	love and marriage	death
....	....	to marry	....
....	....	someone	....

When you find other phrases later on, add them to the table.

~~to marry someone~~ to be born
to be in love with (someone) to die
to fall in love with (someone)
to start school/university
to be keen on (someone) to be dead
to love (someone)
to graduate from university
to have a baby to get married

B Functions

Commenting

1 **Look at the picture. What do you think is happening?**

a She is explaining something to the teacher.
b The teacher is telling her some good news.
c She is telling the teacher something funny.

Now listen to Track 15 and see if you were correct.

2 **Listen to Track 15 again. In what order does Nina (the second speaker) use the following phrases when she listens to her friend's story? Write *1–5* in the boxes.**

Making comments	Exclamations
a I know the feeling. ☐	c How stupid! ☐
b That sounds familiar [1]	d Oh, no! ☐
	e Uh, oh. ☐

3 **Add the following sentences and phrases to the table.**

I know what you mean
How funny! Wow! Really?
No! You're joking!

4 **What does the speaker want to express in each case? Match the expression and the reason the speaker has used it.**

I know what you mean.
~~How funny!~~
Wow! Really? No!
You're joking!
I know the feeling.
That sounds familiar.
How stupid!
Oh, no!
Uh, oh.

a to show amusement
How funny!
b to show sympathy and knowledge of the situation
...
...
...
c to show concern
...
d to show disbelief, surprise or shock
...
...
...
...
...
e to show annoyance or disgust
...

5 Write Bernie's part in the dialogue. Use comments and exclamations from the box. You will not need them all.

~~Let me guess! You lost your mobile phone again, right?~~ Oh, no!
That's nice. Uh, oh. That sounds familiar! How stupid!
I know the feeling. So, buy her more flowers.

ALEX: I did something really stupid.
BERNIE: (a) Let me guess! You lost your mobile phone again, right?
ALEX: No, no. I'm seeing Paula tonight. So I bought her some flowers.
BERNIE: (b) ....
ALEX: Yeah. But I put the flowers on the roof of the car, you know, to open the door.
BERNIE: (c) ....
ALEX: And I drove away with the flowers on the roof. Now I feel really stupid.
BERNIE: (d) ....
ALEX: I don't have money for the cinema <u>and</u> more flowers.
BERNIE: (e) ....

Listen to Track 16 to check your answers.

6 Listen to Track 17. You are Bernie. Read out his words when it's your turn.

7 Follow the instructions in *italics* to write a new dialogue. Use the dialogue in exercise 5 to help you.

YOUR FRIEND: I did something really stupid.
(You think she lost her glasses again.)
YOU: (a) Let me guess! ....

YOUR FRIEND: No. I bought a cake for my sister's birthday.
(You think that's kind.)
YOU: (b) ....

YOUR FRIEND: But I put it on my chair and I sat on it!
(You think that was stupid. Advise her/him to buy another cake.)
YOU: (c) .... !

YOUR FRIEND: I haven't got any more money!
(You have the same problem!)
YOU: (d) .... !

Listen to Track 18 to check your answers.

UNIT 7

A Vocabulary

Activities (and where we do them)

1 **Which of these sports are always held indoors? Tick the boxes.**

football ☐ tennis ☐ baseball ☐ bowling ☑ golf ☐ boxing ☐ pool ☐

2 **Match the sports from exercise 1 with the places in the box. Write labels for the pictures.**

alley ~~course~~ court field pitch ring table

3 **What do sentences *a–g* describe? Write the words from exercises 1 and 2. The first one is done for you.**

a This course has many holes! ....golf course........

b It's a ring but you can't wear it round your finger. ....

c You can't grow plants in this field. ....

d You can't eat your meals sitting at this one! ....

e This has 'singles' and 'doubles' matches. ....

f There are 22 people on this one and 20 want the same ball! ....

g A ball with holes in it? That's what you need here. ....

4 Complete each sentence with all the correct possibilities from the list.

a Do you want to go bowling/sailing/skating ?

bowling sailing skating listening to a concert

b Do you want to go .... ?

swimming shopping cycling watching a film

c Andy came .... with us.

dancing having fun rowing bowling

d Jan didn't want to go to ....

football baseball practice shopping riding

e Do you like riding .... ?

skates horses motorcycles a bicycle

f Matt can play .... very well.

football golf boxing music

5 Match the columns. Then use the words to complete the sentences.

golf	~~court~~
boxing	pitch
~~tennis~~	field
pool	ring
baseball	course
football	table
bowling	alley

a Where can we play tennis?
There's a tennis court near my house.

b Why are there only 21 players on the .... ?
The referee sent one player off.

c The fight is about to begin. The boxers are already in the ....

d How many holes are there on this .... ?
Only nine.

e Is bowling popular here?
Not yet. But they're building a .... in the shopping centre.

f Does San Fernando have a baseball team?
We have a team but we play in San Diego: there is no .... in San Fernando.

g The hotel has three .... in the games room.

WORD BANK

Make a chart like this in your Word Bank notebook. Write the activity words from this unit beside the correct verb in the chart. Can you add any other partners for each verb?

Activity verbs and their partners	
Verbs	**Partners**
go	swimming, shopping
come	
go to	
ride	
play	

B Functions

Inviting

1 Complete each gap in the dialogue with a word or phrase.

MATT: Hi, Liz
LIZ: Hi, Matt.
MATT: Would you like (a) ....to come.... rowing?
LIZ: Rowing?
MATT: Yeah. Rowing. You know. In (b) ....
LIZ: Of course (c) .... 'in a boat'. It's just that, well, you have a (d) ....
MATT: You're right! (e) .... I thought you could (f) .... the actual rowing.
LIZ: Oh no.
MATT: No? (g) .... ?
LIZ: I'm not (h) .... rowing, actually. I'm not (i) .... at it.
MATT: Oh right. Well, how about a walk?
LIZ: I'm a bit tired.
MATT: Or a coffee?
LIZ: Now you're talking!

Listen to Track 19. Did you have the same words and phrases as Matt and Liz?

2 Match the first half of the invitations with the appropriate verbs.

a Do you fancy …
b Do you want to …
c How about …
d Would you like to …

1 go rowing? …
2 going rowing? …

3 Complete the table with the phrases.

~~I'd love to.~~ I'd love to, but … I'd rather not.
I'm not really sure. No thanks. Perhaps.
That would be great. What a fantastic idea!
Why not? Yes, OK. Yes, please.
Now you're talking!

Saying yes	Not sure	Saying no
I'd love to		

4 Listen to Track 20 and complete the table. What do the people invite their friends to do? Write the places or activities in the table. Do their friends say yes, no, or are they not sure? Tick the correct boxes.

People	Place/Activity	Yes	No	Not sure
a Jamie invites Nat	bowling	☐	☑	☐
b Sue invites Sam	1	☐	☐	☐
	2	☐	☐	☐
c Tricia invites Mike	1	☐	☐	☐
	2	☐	☐	☐

5 Listen to Track 20 again and add to the table. Write the expressions they use in the correct boxes.

People	Place/Activity	YYes	No	Not sure
a Jamie invites Nat	bowling Would you like to come bowling?		☑ I'd love to, but I can't.	

6 Use the expressions in the table to invite Mike to the places (in brackets). Then listen to Track 21 and say your lines after the beep.

YOU: (a dance) (**a**) .... ?
MIKE: A dance? Well, I don't really like dancing.
YOU: (a concert) (**b**) .... on Tuesday then?
MIKE: I'd love to, but I'm busy on Tuesday.
YOU: (to dinner) (**c**) .... tomorrow?
MIKE: Now you're talking! Everybody says you're a great cook!

UNIT 8

A Vocabulary

Feelings

1 Write the adjectives under the correct pictures.

angry nervous excited frightened happy in love jealous ~~proud~~ sad

a proud

b ....

c ....

d ....

e ....

f ....

g ....

h ....

i ....

2 Complete the table with words from exercise 1.

Positive feelings	Negative feelings
To be/feel: happy	To be/feel: sad

3 Match the nouns with the adjectives in the same word family.

Nouns		Adjectives
happiness		amused
sadness		angry
nervousness		disappointed
excitement		excited
amusement		frightened
disappointment	be/feel	happy
anger		jealous
pride		nervous
jealousy		proud
fright		sad

Can you find two common endings for nouns in the table?

....

....

4 Write sentences to react to the information. Use words from the table.

a A: My cat died!
B: I'm sorry. You're probably feeling very sad.

b A: Thomas has a job interview tomorrow.
B: He must be ....

c A: Dave won the writing competition.
B: Lucky Dave! I bet he's really ....

d A: Adam and Kate are getting married.
B: Really? I'm sure they'll be ....

e A: Penny's doing her first bungee jump in a minute!
B: She must be ....

f A: Ian accidentally deleted all my work on the computer.
B: Poor you! You must feel really ....

g A: Gina's going out with Laura's ex-boyfriend.
B: Laura's probably .... She's still in love with him.

h A: Millie is going to see Madonna in concert.
B: Millie must be .... Madonna's her favourite singer.

WORD BANK

a Write the adjectives in this section in your Word Bank notebook. Write the situations in exercise 4 to help you remember their meaning.

b Add other situations that are meaningful to you personally.

To be/to feel sad
e.g. when your cat dies.

To be/to feel excited
e.g. when you are going to see your favourite singer.

B Functions

Apologising

1 Listen to Track 22. Match the dialogues with the pictures. Write *1–4*.

a Dialogue ....2....

b Dialogue ....

c Dialogue ....

d Dialogue ....

2 Listen to Track 22 again. Tick the expressions you hear.

Apologising	Responding to apologies
I apologise. ☐	Apology accepted. ☐
I apologise for being late. ☐	That's all right. ☐
Sorry! ☑	That's OK. ☐
I'm sorry that you waited so long. ☐	Never mind. ☐
I didn't mean to upset you. ☐	Not at all. ☐
	Don't worry about it. ☐

3 Formal or informal?

Listen to Track 23. Match the dialogues with the pictures.

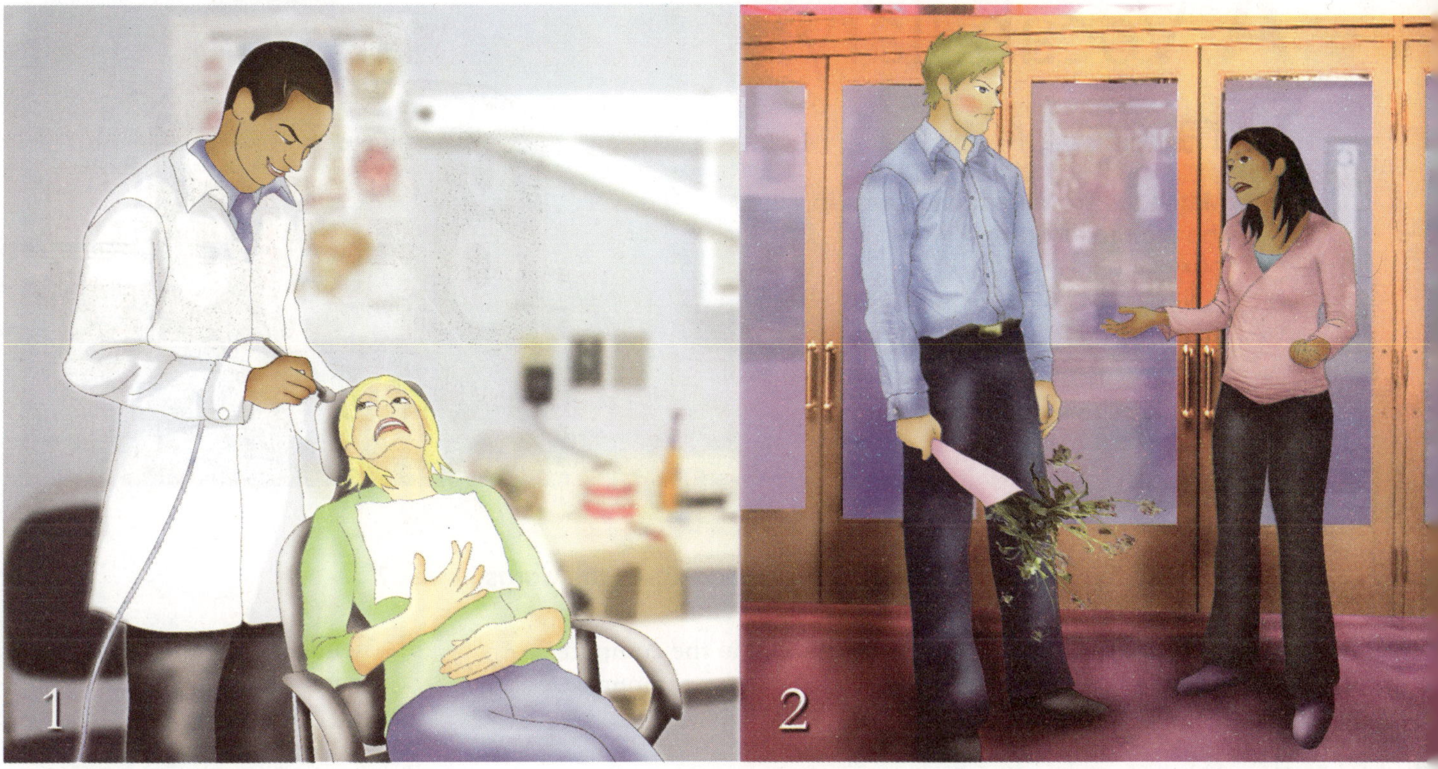

1 Dialogue .... 2 Dialogue ....

4 Listen to Track 23 again. Write the apologies in the spaces.

Dialogue a

A: You're late!

B: Sorry!

A: Well, we said 8 o'clock and it's 8.45 now.

B: I know. (**a**) ....

A: It wasn't much fun, you know?

B: (**b**) .... I lost my laptop. That's why I'm late.

A: Oh, I'm really sorry. (**c**) .... Listen, do you still want to see the film?

Dialogue b

A: Good afternoon, Mr Rice. (**d**) ....

B: Yes, I see your appointment was at four.

A: (**e**) .... There was a lot of traffic.

B: Well, never mind. Now, open wide please.

A: Ouch!

B: Oops, (**f**) .... Did that hurt?

5 Listen again to Dialogue a on Track 24. You are B. Respond when it's your turn.

UNIT 9

A Vocabulary

Phrasal verbs

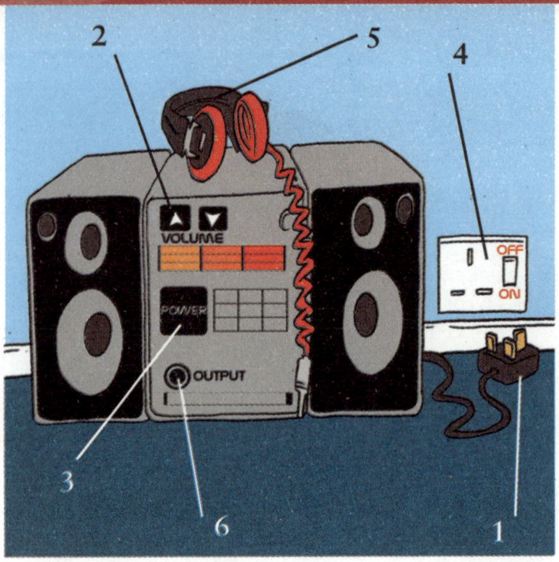

1 Match the words and the items in the picture. Write *1–6* in the boxes.

a socket [4] d plug [ ]
b headset [ ] e volume control [ ]
c power button [ ] f output [ ]

2 Look at the sentences. What do you notice about the words in blue?

Turn on the television. Or Turn the television on.

Plug in the computer. Or Plug the computer in.

Switch off the printer. Or Switch the printer off.

3 Which words go together? Tick the table.

	the TV	the computer	the headset	the light	the radio	the volume
plug in	✓	✓	✓	✓	✓	
switch on/off						
turn on/off						
turn up/down						

4 Give advice in answer to these comments. Use phrasal verbs from the table in exercise 3.

a The music is too loud! Turn down the volume.
b I can't hear what the people on the radio are saying. ....
c I'm bored with this game. ....
d I can't see anything! ....
e I don't want everybody to hear the CD. ....
f I want to watch my new TV. Where do I start? ....
g I plugged in the CD player and I turned it on but nothing is happening! ....

5 Match the beginning of the sentences in column 1 with the correct endings in column 2.

a Put on the headset.
b ....
c ....
d ....
e ....
f ....
g ....

Column 1	Column 2
a Put on	1 the volume. I can't hear anything.
b Switch off	2 the phone. I'm busy.
c Turn up	3 the light when you go.
d Turn on	4 the printer before you use it.
e Turn off	5 the TV. The programme is starting!
f Plug in	6 the computer when you finish.
g Pick up	7 the headset. We don't want to listen to your music.

6 Rewrite the sentences you made in exercise 5, changing the place of the preposition.

a Put the headset on.
b ....
c ....
d ....
e ....
f ....
g ....

7 Complete these sentences with a phrasal verb from exercise 5.

a Please turn up the volume. I want to hear the weather forecast.
b Did you remember to .... the DVD player when you left?
c Why don't you .... the lamp? It's too dark here.
d .... your coat. It's cold out there!
e You don't have to .... this radio. It's got batteries.
f Can you .... the answering machine? I want to listen to my messages.

WORD BANK

Make a chart that starts like this in your Word Bank notebook. Write the phrasal verbs in this unit in the chart with the words that go with them.

Phrasal verbs	Words that go with them	Special grammar
Put on	your headset, a coat,	Put your headset on.

Add as many words as you can to the second column.

B Functions

Making phone calls

1 **Put these two conversations in the correct order. Write numbers *1–6* or *1–7* in the boxes.**

a

- ☐ Bye.
- ☐ Hi, Sue. It's Harry. Is Milly there?
- [1] Hello.
- ☐ No, that's OK. I'll call her later.
- ☐ OK. See you.
- ☐ No, she's out. Do you want me to say you called?

b

- [1] Hello, Language Centre. Can I help you?
- ☐ Yes, I'll hold.
- ☐ Sorry to keep you waiting. The line is still engaged. Can I take a message?
- ☐ Could you put me through to Mr Rose?
- ☐ I'm sorry. The line is busy. Would you like to hold?
- ☐ Yes. Could you tell Mr Rose that Harry Parker called? It's about his DVD player.
- ☐ Of course.

Listen to Track 25. Check your answers.

2 **Complete the table with phrases from the dialogue.**

Making phone calls	Formal	Informal
Offering help		
Making a request		
Asking to speak to someone	Can/Could I speak to ...? I'd like to speak to	Is Milly there?

3 **Complete the phone call.**

You are phoning a shop where you bought an MP3 player. It doesn't work. You want your money back.

SHOP: Hello. Best Electronics. Can I help you?
YOU: (*ask to speak to the manager*) Could you ... .
SHOP: Who's calling please?
YOU: (*introduce yourself*) ....
SHOP: Sorry, his line's engaged.
YOU: (*ask her to take a message*) ....
SHOP: Sure.
YOU: (*leave a message*) ....

4 **Listen to Track 26.**

Who does Marcial want to speak to? ....

Why can't Chris speak to Steve? ....

....

....

5 **Listen to Track 26 again. Write:**

a three ways of answering the phone Hello? Best Electronics. ....

....

b three ways to ask to speak to someone ....

....

c an expression that means 'Can you wait?' ....

....

6 **Complete the rest of the phone call. Then listen to Track 27 and read out your lines when it's your turn.**

YOU: (*answering the phone*) Hello. .... ?
FRANCES: Hi. This is Frances. Can I speak to Carmen, please?
YOU: (*say she is not in*) ....
FRANCES: When will she be back?
YOU: (*you are not sure – offer to take a message*) .... ?
FRANCES: Yes, please. Tell her Frances called. Can she meet me outside the cinema at 8.30, not at 8? I can't be there earlier.
YOU: (*read out the message*) ....
FRANCES: That's right. Who's speaking please?
YOU: (*say who you are*) ....
FRANCES: OK. Thanks for your help. Bye.

UNIT 10

A Vocabulary

Giving and receiving

1 Match the words and phrases in the box with the pictures.

~~cash~~	cheque	
credit card	gold watch	
receipt	shop assistant	
to the shops	unwrapping	
wrapping up		

a ....cash....
b ....
c ....
d ....
e ....
f ....
g ....
h ....
i ....

2 Match the beginnings of the sentences in column A with the endings in column B.

A	B
a He changed it ...	1 a gold watch.
b Peter ...	2 by credit card.
c Later, Peter took ...	3 cash.
d Lucy went ...	4 for her friend Peter.
e She asked for a ...	5 pay by cheque.
f She chose ...	6 receipt.
g She didn't ...	7 to Peter.
h She didn't pay in ...	8 to the shops.
i She gave the watch ...	9 wrapped up the watch.
j She paid ...	10 unwrapped the present.
k She was looking for something ...	11 the watch back to the shop.
l The shop assistant ...	12 for something else.

a ....12.... g ....
b .... h ....
c .... i ....
d .... j ....
e .... k ....
f .... l ....

3 Write the sentences in the correct sequence.

a Lucy went to the shops.
b ....
c ....
d ....
e ....
f ....
g ....
h ....
i ....
j ....
k ....
l ....

4 Look at the picture and complete the sentences with the words in the box.

change gave receipt

A Good morning. Can I help you?
B Yes. My mother (**a**) gave me this present for my birthday and I'd like to (**b**) .... it, please.
A (**c**) .... it?
B Yes, (**d**) .... it for something bigger.
A That should be possible. Do you have the (**e**) .... ?
B The (**f**) .... ?
A Yes, first I need the (**g**) ...., then you can (**h**) .... it.
B Ah, well …

WORD BANK

In your Word Bank notebook, make a list of all the different things you can give as presents for these occasions.

wedding engagement birthday Mother's day Father's day

B Functions

Thanking people

1 **Listen to Track 28. Which is the correct picture?** ....

a

b

c

d

2 **Listen to Track 28 again. Complete the dialogue.**

JANE: I just want to (a) say thank you .

CARL: You're (b) ....

JANE: No, really. You (c) ....

CARL: It was (d) ....

JANE: No, really. Thanks to you it was (e) ....

CARL: (f) .... a relief.

JANE: Seriously, thank you (g) ....

CARL: Sure.

3 **Read through the following phrases and decide whether they are thanks because …**

1 someone did something for you.
2 someone gave you something.
3 someone helped you.

Write *1–3* in the boxes. Note: There is sometimes more than one suitable answer.

a It's just what I wanted. [2]

b It's really kind of you. ☐

c Many thanks for .... ☐

d Thank you for all your help/everything you've done for me. ☐

e Thank you so much for ....ing .... ☐

f Thanks a lot. ☐

g Thanks to you the .... was a great success. ☐

h You've saved my life! Thanks. ☐

4 **Put these words in the correct order to make sentences. Use capital letters where necessary.**

a just / I / wanted / it's / what It's just what I wanted.

you / I'm / it / like / glad ....

b all / you / for / help / your / thank ....

welcome / you're ....

c party / success / a / you / to / thanks / the / great / was ....

a / was / pleasure / it ....

d me / so / thanks / helping / homework / much / with / for / my ....

problem / no ....

e for / thanks / lot / dinner / a ....

it / mention / don't ....

Now listen to Track 29 and check your answers.

5 **Now match each dialogue with a picture. Write the number in the boxes.**

6 **Imagine you are in these situations. Write what you would say.**

a It's your birthday and your friend gave you a CD of your favourite band.

....

....

b It's your friend's birthday and she thanks you for the DVD that you gave her.

....

....

c Your brother helped you to fix your bicycle.

....

....

d Your mother cooked you a delicious dinner.

....

....

Now listen to Track 30 and speak when it's your turn.

UNIT 11

A Vocabulary

Performance

1 Read the paragraph and choose the correct photograph.

Last week I read a review in the newspaper. It was about a new play called *Blue Name*. It said the play was very moving. The reviewer cried at the end, he said. I rang the theatre and booked a ticket. I went to see the play. I got a good seat so I had a good view of the stage. When the curtain went up I was very excited, but unfortunately the play was very boring. It was so slow, and I didn't cry at all! But at the end of the performance everyone in the audience clapped and clapped. So maybe there's something wrong with me!

a

b

The correct photograph is ....

2 Find words in blue in the text which mean:

a a piece of writing about a play or a film ....review....

b large piece of material between the stage and the audience ....

c not exciting ....

d not fast ....

e put their hands together ....

f show/play ....

g the place where the actors are ....

h bought/ordered a ticket before the show ....

i it makes you feel very emotional – a good thing ....

3 Complete the sentences with one of these words.

~~review~~	book	curtain	play	performance
audience	clapped	stage		

a I read a ..review.. of the movie. It said that the movie was excellent.

b Do we need to .... tickets?

c The actors were already on the .... when we arrived late.

d There was a huge .... at the theatre on opening night. There was not one empty seat.

e The .... went up at the beginning of the show and came down at the end.

f There's a .... in this theatre tonight, and tomorrow there's a concert.

g The people watching .... for ten minutes at the end of the show.

h The actors were fantastic in the first .... of Shakespeare's *Romeo and Juliet* last night.

4 Look at these film posters. Then listen to Track 31. Which film are they talking about in each case?

Conversation a ...3...

Conversation b ....

Conversation c ....

Conversation d ....

5 Now imagine you have seen the films. Write your opinions when your friend asks you:

Have you seen *Days of Laughter*?

a ....

Have you seen *Night of the Zombie Killers*?

b ....

Have you seen *The Long Hot Summer*?

c ....

Have you seen *The New York Race*?

d ....

Now listen to Track 32 and answer when it's your turn.

WORD BANK

Which of the words in this vocabulary section refer to films, plays or both?

Make a diagram like this in your Word Bank notebook and write the words in the right place.

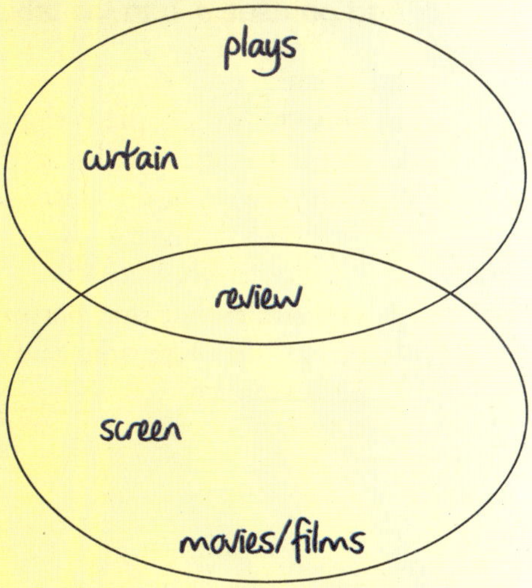

B Functions

Booking tickets, tables, rooms

1 **Write the following questions in the gaps in the dialogue.**

Can you give me your credit card number?
How many tickets would you like?
Is there anything else I can do for you?
~~What time do you want to see the film?~~
Where would you like to sit?

WOMAN: Arts Cinema. Can I help you?
MAN: Yes please. I'd like some tickets for *The Cuba File*, please. For today.
WOMAN: OK. (a) What time do you want to see the film?
MAN: 6.20.
WOMAN: And (b) ....
MAN: Two, please.
WOMAN: (c) ....
MAN: Could we have an aisle seat at the back?
WOMAN: Yes I think I can do that. (d) ....
MAN: Sure. It's 4552 ...
WOMAN: OK sir, the payment's gone through. Come along 15 minutes before the performance starts and your tickets will be here.
MAN: Great.
WOMAN: (e) ....
MAN: No thanks, that's all. Goodbye.

Now listen to Track 33. Were you correct?

2 **Add phrases *a–o* to the table on page 49.**

a At the front. ✓
b How many people is that for?
c In the middle, somewhere.
d I think we can do that.
e I'd like a room for two nights.
f I'd like to book a table.
g I'm afraid that that performance is sold out.
h I'm afraid there aren't any tickets left for that performance.
i I'm afraid we're full tomorrow.
j I'm sorry, sir. The hotel is full on March 19th.
k Not too near the back.
l That's fine.
m We look forward to seeing you on Thursday.
n What dates are you thinking of?
o When is that for?

Function	Examples
Offering a service:	*Can I help you?*
Saying what you want:	
Asking for details:	
Saying it's possible/not possible:	
Getting a credit card number:	*Can you give me your credit card number?*
Saying what the customer should do:	*Come along 15 minutes before the performance starts.*
Ending the conversation:	
Describing where:	*At the front*

Conversation 2

a Oh dear. What about tomorrow? ☐
b Certainly sir. Can I have your credit card number? ☐
c Yes. It's 6475 7564 … ☐
d Two nights? Is that for tonight? ☐
e OK, can I book that room, please? ☐
f We have one room available tomorrow. ☐
g Yes, tonight and tomorrow night. ☐
h The Garden Hotel. Can I help you? 1
i Yes, I'd like a room for two nights, please. ☐
j I'm afraid the hotel is full tonight. ☐

3 Put these two conversations in order. Number the boxes.

Conversation 1

a OK, Ms Healey. Next Wednesday at 8 o'clock, table for two. ☐
b Just for two. ☐
c Thank you very much. ☐
d Jennifer Healey. ☐
e Hello. I'd like to book a table, please. ☐
f 8 p.m. Right. And what's your name? ☐
g Two people on Wednesday. OK, and what time were you thinking of? ☐
h 8 o'clock. ☐
i Murray's restaurant here. 1
j Next Wednesday, please. ☐
k Sure. And how many people is that for? ☐
l Certainly. What day is that for? ☐

Listen to Track 34 and check your answers.

4 Now listen to Track 35. Imagine you are the woman on the phone to the restaurant, and then the man in the hotel. You can change information if you want. Speak when it is your turn.

A Vocabulary

Word families

1 Use your dictionary to complete these tables with words from the same word family.

Verbs	Nouns
clone	
	protection
cook	
move	
	defence

Nouns	Adjectives
	employed, unemployed
plant	
	interested
inspiration	
destruction	

2 Use the correct form of the words from exercise 1 in the sentences below.

a The young woman was happy to be part of an important .... to save wild animals.

b That woman is an .... to young people today. They see her and they want to be like her.

c I love to try new recipes. What about you? Do you like .... ?

d I have several .... in my house. I have to give them plenty of water and take care of them.

e What do you do in your free time? Do you have any .... , like movies or sports?

f My brother doesn't have a job at the moment, he's looking for ....

g After the storm the beach house was completely ....

h Can you help me to .... this piano? It's very heavy.

3 Circle the correct word in blue to complete these paragraphs.

Shawn Fanning (born in 1980) was just 18 years old when he started 'Napster' – a way to share music files over the Internet for free – without paying. Fanning was a university student when he became (**a**) interested/interesting/interest in the Internet. He left university to (**b**) move/movement/moved to California and start his business.

Today Fanning owns a company called SNOCAP. This company (**c**) protects/protection/protected the rights of people who write music – the opposite of his early days with Napster!

Arundhati Roy was born in 1961. She is a writer and (**d**) active/activist from Bengal, India. Her first novel took her five years to write and it is called *The God of Small Things*.

Today Roy travels the world giving (**e**) speak/spoken/speeches about the environment and justice and she is an (**f**) inspire/inspiration to the people who meet her.

She is (**g**) marriage/marry/married to a film-maker and lives in Delhi.

4 Complete this word family table.

Verb	Noun	Adjective
XXXXXXXX	scientist/science	scientific
discover	discovery	
		interested (in)
	destruction	
XXXXXXXX	environment/	
	plant	
protect		
		married
move		
act/		active

5 Use the words from the table in exercise 4 to complete these sentences.

a My sister's favourite subject at school is ......science...... and when she grows up she wants to be an ....

b This factory is causing a lot of .... damage.

c The .... of the rainforest is dangerous for the .... , because the rainforest affects the weather.

d It is important that we .... more trees in the world.

c The .... of radium was important for medicine.

f Many important .... in the world .... wild animals.

g The couple got .... last year. The .... took place at the beach.

WORD BANK

Make a table like this in your Word Bank notebook.

Write ten word families that you know in the table.

Verb	Noun	Adjective
rescue	rescue, rescuer	rescued

B Functions

Offering to help

1 **Match the two parts of the conversations.**

a ...3...
b ....
c ....
d ....
e ....

Listen to Track 36. Were you correct?

a **Why don't you let me** carry your bags?
b I don't think I can reach the button.
c **Would you like some help** with your homework?
d **Can I help you** to finish those forms?
e **Shall I** make you something to eat?

1 **Thanks.** I need to get home early tonight.
2 **Don't worry about it. I'm fine.** I ate about an hour ago.
3 They are very heavy. **Thanks.**
4 **Allow me.** I'll press it for you.
5 **No, thanks. I can do it by myself.**

2 **Where did the conversations take place? Choose phrases from the box.**

a Conversation a at the supermarket
b Conversation b ....
c Conversation c ....
d Conversation d ....
e Conversation e ....

at home ~~at the supermarket~~
at the office in a lift at school

3 **Complete the table with the phrases in bold from the conversations in exercise 1.**

Offering help	Why don't you let me ...?
Accepting help	That would be great.
Refusing help	

4 **Complete the dialogues with these words and phrases. Use capital letters where necessary.**

can I	thanks
~~would you like~~	don't worry
allow me	why don't
would be	sure
can you	how about

a A: Would you like me to help you with dinner?

B: Thanks. That .... great. .... chop those onions?

b A: You look tired. .... if I make you a nice cup of tea?

B: .... , dear. I'm fine. I'll have some tea later.

c A: I can't open this door.

B: .... It is very heavy.

d A: .... you do the first part of the reading and I'll do the second part, so we save time?

B: .... It's about 100 pages altogether.

e A: .... help you to do the shopping?

B: .... about it. I only need to get a few things.

Now listen to Track 37 and check your answers.

5 **Complete the dialogues for these situations.**

a Would you like me to help you, son?

....

....

b Wow! What a mess! How about if we help you to get the room ready?

....

....

Now listen to Track 38 and speak when it's your turn.

UNIT 13

A Vocabulary

Abilities

1 **Write the name of the person who has each of these talents or abilities.**

a ....Emily........ is very **sporty**. She loves sports, especially basketball and volleyball, and she's very good at them.

b .... is very **practical**. She does all the things that need doing around the house.

c .... is so **creative**. He can make anything into something else.

d .... likes to meet people at parties. He's very **sociable**.

e .... has **'green fingers'**. Any plant in her garden grows.

f .... is very good at listening and helping his friends. He's an **understanding** person.

2 **Put these letters in the right order to make words to describe abilities and talents.**

a tropsy ....sporty..........
b tansingdreund ..u..........
c carpclati ..p..........
d blecioas ..s..........
e nonfidcet ..c..........
f recavite ..c..........
g trisacit ..a..........
h gillaco ..l..........

3 **Now match the words *a–h* above to the definitions *1–8*.**

1 You are good at working things out step by step.
2 You like meeting people and being with friends.
3 You are good at art, like drawing and painting.
4 You have good original ideas.
5 You are not shy and you are very sure of yourself.
6 You are a good listener and think about other people's feelings.
7 You like playing sports.
8 You can fix things and you don't panic in a crisis.

a ..7.. b .... c .... d .... e ....
f .... g .... h ....

4 **Complete these advertisements with a suitable word or expression.**

a **Do you have** ..green fingers.. **?**
We need someone to help us once a week in our garden. We grow mostly flowers and some vegetables.
Call us on 9384973

b I'm looking for a .... person to help me keep my books. I need someone who can go through all my receipts and information and organise it for me.
Mrs Murphy 7849504

c We are looking for an .... person to help us draw posters for a concert next month.
Contact: Josie

d Do you have great ideas? Can you make something out of nothing? Then you might be the .... person we are looking for.
Call John at 6748392

e We need a .... person who loves to meet other people and loves parties. We are professional party organisers.
Write to: Suzie
Contact@greatparties.com

f Are you .... ?
Do you love to play games?
Come and try out for our new basketball team.
We need you!
Come to the gym on Friday at 2 p.m.

WORD BANK

Write the names of ten people you know. Use the new words from this unit to describe them in your Word Bank notebook.

Example: My dad: sporty, practical, sociable

B Functions

Asking for language help

1 Put this conversation in order. Write the numbers *1–9* in the boxes.

a RACHEL: Oh yes, that's it. A barrister. ☐

b RACHEL: I'm not sure yet. ☐

c JAKE: Oh, it's the study of all things connected with crime and criminals. ☐

d JAKE: No, I'm not going to be a barrister. I'm going to be a criminology teacher. What about you? What are you going to study? ☐

e JAKE: I'm going to study criminology at university. ☐

f RACHEL: Oh, that sounds interesting. So are you going to be someone who goes to court? What do you call it? ☐

g RACHEL: Criminology? What's that? ☐

h JAKE: A barrister? ☐

i RACHEL: What are you going to do when you leave school? [1]

Now listen to Track 39 and check your answers.

2 Complete the dialogue with one of these words or expressions. You will need to use some of them more than once.

mean	say
what's	call
means	

KRISTINA: Ellie, what does 'talent' (a) ......mean...... ?

ELLIE: Oh, it (b) .... something that you are good at.

KRISTINA: OK, I understand. Like I have a talent for singing?

ELLIE: That's right.

KRISTINA: And what do you (c) .... it when you like doing something, even if you are not good at it?

ELLIE: You (d) .... , like a hobby?

KRISTINA: Yes, a hobby.

ELLIE: Usually people who have hobbies have some kind of ability for the thing they like to do, but not always.

KRISTINA: What do you (e) .... by 'ability'?

ELLIE: Ability means being able to do something, like an activity.

KRISTINA: Activity? (f) .... that?

ELLIE: An activity is something you do.

KRISTINA: Wow! I need a dictionary. Then I could find these words for myself. How do you (g) ....'find out something for yourself'?

ELLIE: Discover. Yes, I think you need a dictionary, Kristina.

Now listen to Track 40 and check your answers.

3 Complete these questions.

a What ......do...... you ......mean...... by discipline?

b 'Attention'? What's .... ?

c What .... 'comfortable' .... ?

d How .... 'not calm', 'running around', 'acting crazy'?

e What .... when something makes you feel afraid?

4 Now match questions *a–e* to these answers.

1 Wild.

2 It means you feel at ease, relaxed.

3 It frightens you.

4 It's when you have strict rules.

5 It's when someone talks to you and takes notice of what you do.

a ....4.... b .... c .... d .... e ....

5 Complete this dialogue by writing the correct question from the box.

How do you call it
What does that mean
How do you say this
~~What do you call it~~

ABBY: I really don't like parties. (**a**) ......What do you call it...... when you don't like to meet people?

CHRIS: Shy? Are you shy?

ABBY: Yes, I am. (**b**) .... when something makes you feel afraid?

CHRIS: You mean, it frightens you.

ABBY: Yes, that's right.

CHRIS: That's strange, because you're very popular.

ABBY: Popular? (**c**) .... ?

CHRIS: It's when a lot of people like you.

ABBY: Yes, I think I'm popular, but I don't like it when people take notice of me? (**d**) .... ?

CHRIS: Oh, you mean when people pay you a lot of attention.

ABBY: That's right. I like to stay by myself.

Now listen to Track 41 and read Abby's part after each beep.

UNIT 14

A Vocabulary

Describing the size of things

1 Use the words to describe the pictures.

a ......minute......

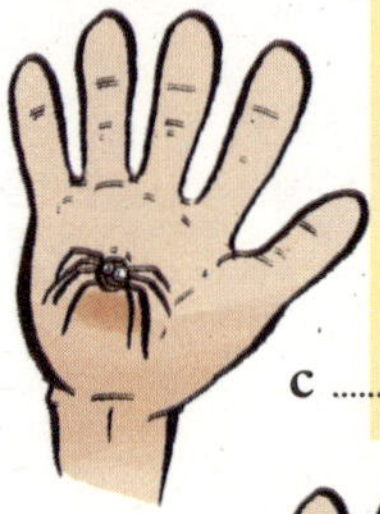

c ....

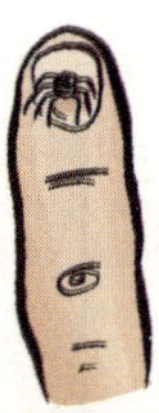

b ....

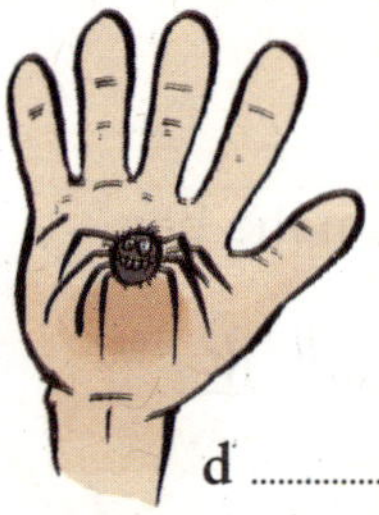

d ....

e ....

g ....

f ....

h ....

big	enormous	gigantic	huge
large	~~minute~~	small	tiny

2 Look at the picture of the swimming pool and answer the questions.

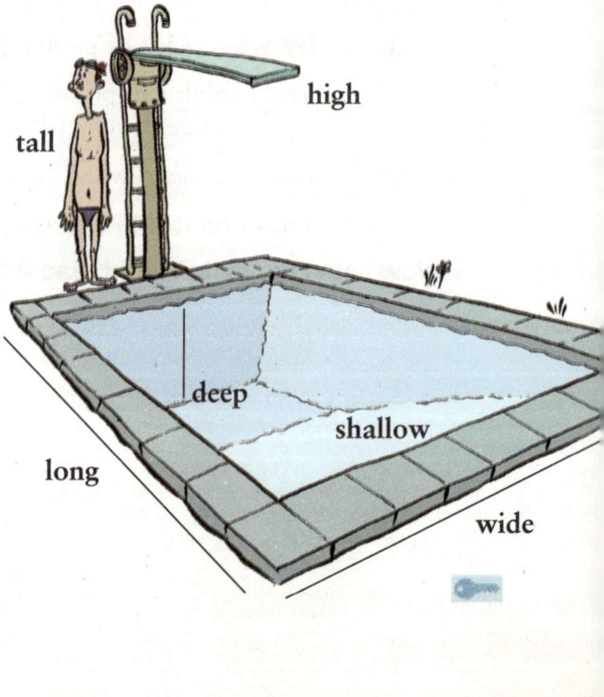

a Which words in the picture are the opposite of:

low ......high......

narrow ....

short ....

b Which words are used to describe 'thin' things (trees, buildings, etc.)? ....

c Which words are used to describe 'wide' things (mountains, walls, ceilings, etc.)? ....

d Which words can describe rivers, lakes and oceans?

....

e Which words can be used for rooms or houses?

....

3 Unjumble these words to find adjectives that describe size.

a raleg	large	e ibg	....
b sonoreum	....	f tangicig	....
c nimetu	....	g lamsl	....
d ytni	....	h guhe	....

4 Now put the words in order of size along this diagram.

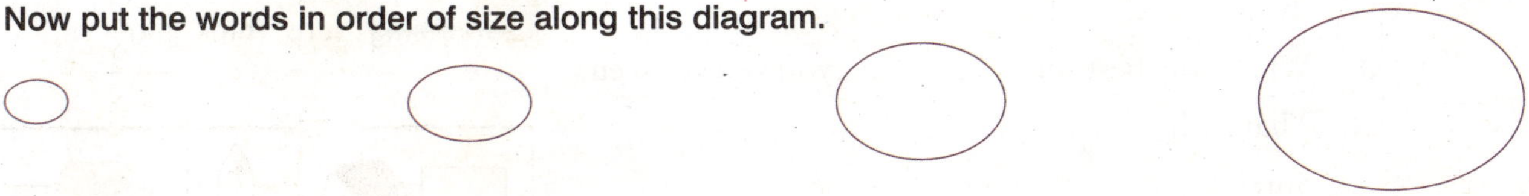

a minute c .... e .... g ....

b .... d .... f .... h ....

5 Look at the pictures and complete the sentences with one of these words.

wide   wide   high   tall   deep   ~~shallow~~

a The water is shallow.

b The road is very ....

c This tree is very ....

d The road is not very ....

e The woman is very ....

f This hole is very ....

WORD BANK

In your Word Bank notebook write one thing you know that is:

minute tiny small big large huge enormous gigantic long wide high tall deep shallow

Example:

minute – This writing is minute. I can't read it.

B Functions

Comparing experiences

1 Complete the dialogue with words from the box.

about difficult easy film know right ~~something~~ sure think too

ANNE: Can I ask you (a) something ?
CATH: (b) ....
ANNE: What's the best (c) .... you've ever seen?
CATH: That's (d) ....
ANNE: Sorry.
CATH: No, that's all (e) .... The best film? I (f) .... it's *The Usual Suspects*. I saw it on TV last week. What (g) .... you?
ANNE: That's easy. *Jaws*. You (h) .... , the one with the great white shark.
CATH: Yes, I liked that (i) ....
ANNE: I've seen it about 15 times!

Now listen to Track 42. Were you correct?

2 Practise saying the dialogue. Can you do it from memory?

3 Make questions, using the noun phrases with appropriate verbs from the box.

been to eaten had read seen

a beautiful thing What's the most beautiful thing you've ever seen?

b delicious food ....

c boring book ....

d frightening experience ....

e good concert ....

f horrible food ....

g ugly thing ....

Now answer the questions.

4 **Put these words in order to make sentences and questions. Use capital letters where necessary.**

a your / take / time /

Take your time.

b sounds / that / nice /

....

c made / chicken / with / she / gravy / and / roast / roast / potatoes /

....

d have / I'll / think / to /

....

e loved / yes, / it / everyone /

....

f the / eaten / what's / delicious / ever / you've / most / meal /

....

g she / did / cook / what /

....

h birthday / 18th / mum / the / it / for / my / was / meal / cooked / my /

....

5 **Now put the sentences in order to make a short conversation.**

1 ....f.... 2 .... 3 .... 4 ....

5 .... 6 .... 7 .... 8 ....

Listen to Track 43 to check your answers.

6 **Now answer these questions about yourself.**

What was the most delicious meal you've ever eaten?

....

Who cooked it?

....

What did that person 'or people' cook?

....

Now listen to Track 44 and speak when it's your turn.

A Vocabulary

Head and face

1 **Look at the pictures and label them with the words in the box. Use a dictionary if necessary.**

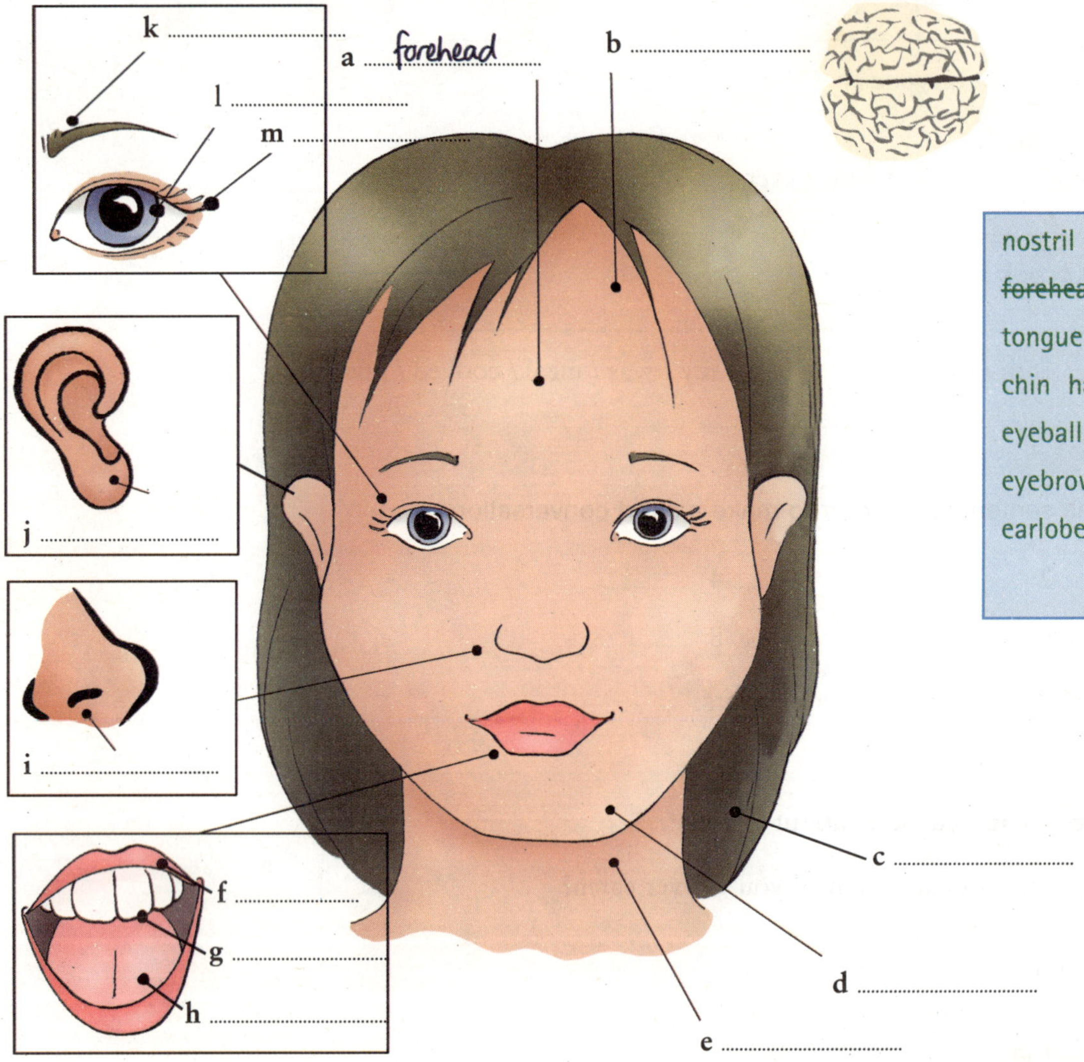

nostril brain
~~forehead~~
tongue neck
chin hair
eyeball lips
eyebrow teeth
earlobe eyelashes

2 **What part(s) of your head and face do you use to do these things?**

a smile mouth,
b speak ....
c laugh ....
d wink ....
e blink ....
f think ....
g hear ....
h listen to music ....
i see ....
j smell ....
k taste ....

3 Now test yourself. Look at these pictures. Can you identify the parts of the head and face? Write the word.

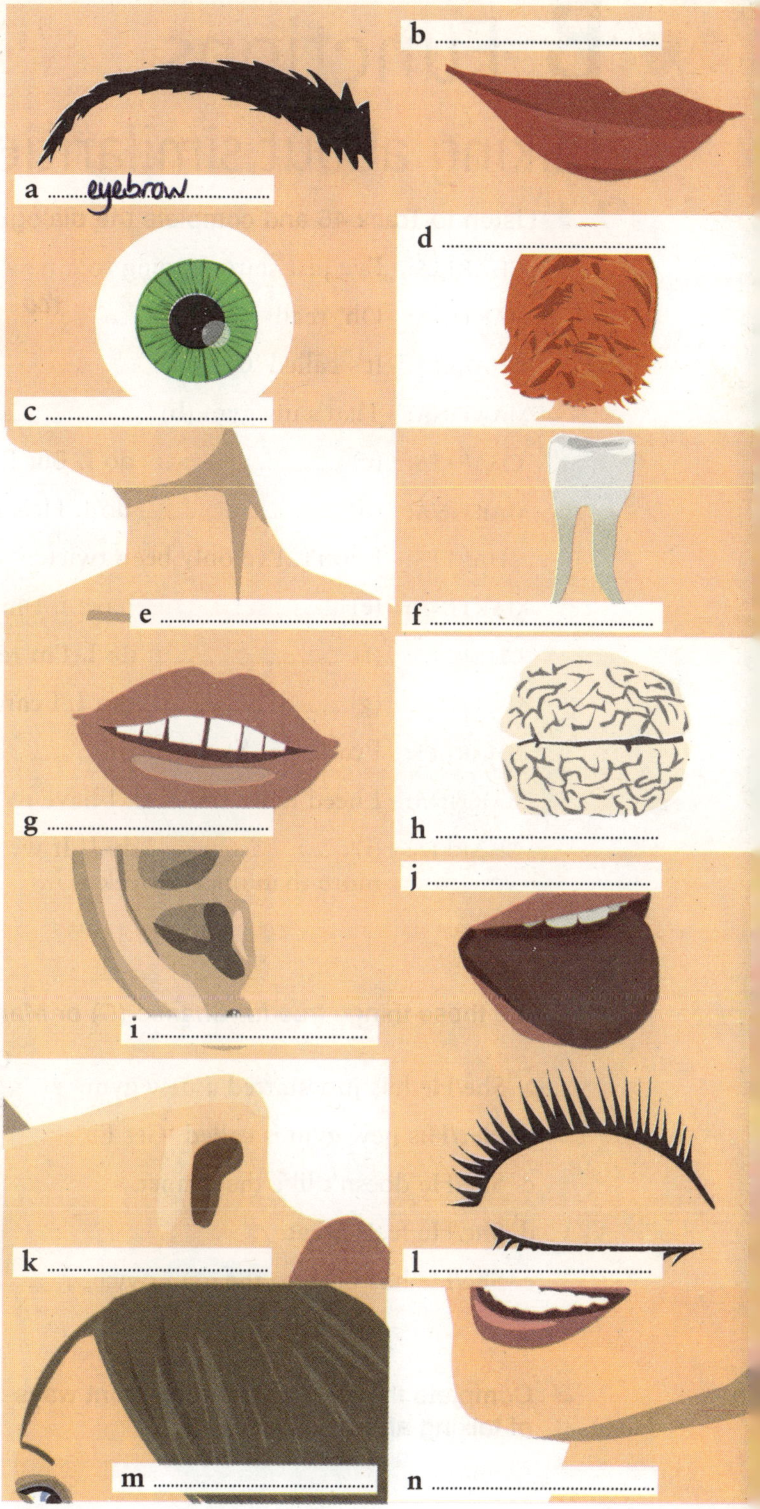

4 Use one of the words from exercise 3 to complete these sentences.

a You need your teeth .... to bite something.
b People often wear earrings on their ....
c Your .... protect your eyes.
d The holes in your nose are called ....
e Your .... is at the bottom of your face.
f We use our .... to kiss.
g It's very long – I need to cut my ....
h The top of your head is called your ....
i Your .... are above your eyes.
j If you wear contact lenses, you wear them in your ....
k You need your .... to speak and to taste.
l Your head rests on top of your ....
m You need your .... to think.

WORD BANK

In your Word Bank notebook draw a picture of the head and face and label all the parts that you know. Now write all the verbs you know that use parts of the head and face next to the parts you use.

Mouth: talk, eat, smile, etc.

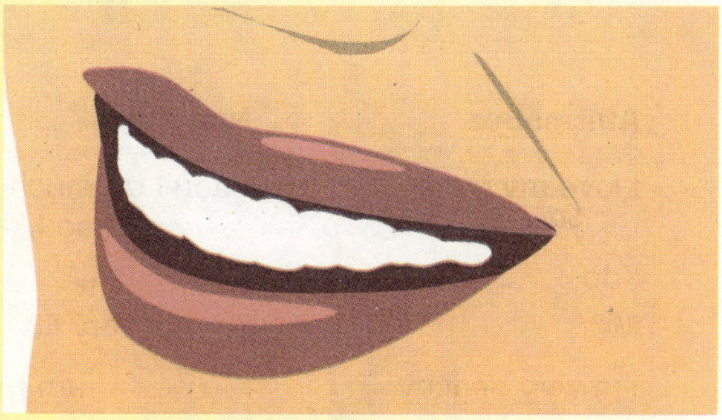

B Functions

Talking about similarities and differences

1 Listen to Track 45 and complete the dialogue with the words in the box.

too	so	either	neither

CHARLES: I've just started going to a new gym.
MARTINA: Oh, really? Me (a) ......too...... . Which gym?
CHARLES: It's called 'Get Fit'.
MARTINA: That's my gym (b) .... I love it.
CHARLES: (c) .... do I. But I don't like the trainer.
MARTINA: (d) .... do I. He's unfriendly, but I feel great.
CHARLES: I don't. I've only been twice.
MARTINA: (e) .... have I. I just don't have the time.
CHARLES: (f) .... do I. I'm really busy at work.
MARTINA: (g) .... am I. I can't go to the gym today.
CHARLES: I can't go (h) .... I have to work late.
MARTINA: I need more time off. I have to talk to my boss.
CHARLES: (i) .... do I! If we want to get healthy, we'll need to go to the gym more than once a week!

2 Are these things true for *Charles* (*C*) or *Martina* (*M*), or both of them? Tick the right columns.

	C	M
a She/He has just started a new gym.	✓	✓
b Her/His new gym is called 'Get Fit'.		
c She/He doesn't like the trainer.		
d She/He feels great.		
e She/He has been to the gym twice.		
f She/He doesn't have enough time to go to the gym.		
g She/He is really busy at work.		
h She/He can't go to the gym today.		
i She/He needs to talk to her/his boss.		

3 Complete the table with the different ways of talking about similarities.

Affirmative	Negative
I love my gym. ......So...... do I. I do, ... Me	I don't do much exercise. .... do I. I don't, ...
I'm very healthy. .... am I. I am, ... Me	I'm not very fit. .... am I. I'm not, ...

4 Complete this conversation with the phrases from the box.

Neither can I.
I do, too.
Me too!
I'm not either.
~~So do I.~~
Neither do I.

RICHARD: I need to wear glasses.

ALICE: (a) ....So do I.... . I can't read the newspaper very well.

RICHARD: (b) .... It gives me a headache.

ALICE: (c) .... But I don't know any good opticians.

RICHARD: (d) .... , but my sister knows one.

ALICE: That's good. Can you give me the name when you've asked her?

RICHARD: Sure. I need to have my eyes tested soon.

ALICE: (e) .... Call me tonight, I'm not going out.

RICHARD: (f) .... I'll call you around seven.

ALICE: OK. Thanks.

Now listen to Track 46 and check your answers.

5 Look at this information about Maria and Claire and write appropriate sentences about their similarities and differences.

a Maria's last name is Smith.

....So is Claire's....

b Claire is from London.

....

c Maria is a student.

....

d Claire is studying medicine.

....

e Claire isn't married.

....

f Maria lives in Wimbledon.

....

Name:	Maria Smith
Age:	22
Occupation:	Psychology student
Marital status:	Single
Hometown:	London
Address:	15 High St, Wimbledon

Name:	Claire Smith
Age:	22
Occupation:	Medical student
Marital status:	Single
Hometown:	London
Address:	26 Merton Court, Wimbledon

6 Now complete this short dialogue between Maria and Claire.

MARIA: Hi, my name's Maria Smith.

CLAIRE: My name's Smith, (a) ....too.... .

MARIA: Oh really? Where are you from?

CLAIRE: I'm from London.

MARIA: (b) .... ! Where do you live?

CLAIRE: In Wimbledon.

MARIA: (c) .... Are you married?

CLAIRE: No, I'm (d) ....

MARIA: (e) .... I. What do you do?

CLAIRE: I'm a student.

MARIA: (f) .... What are you studying?

CLAIRE: Medicine. Are you studying medicine, (g) .... ?

MARIA: No, (h) .... I'm studying psychology.

Listen to Track 47 and speak at the 'beep'.

UNIT 16

A Vocabulary

From strange to amazing

1 Read these paragraphs and put the words in blue into the word map.

This is a strange creature with two creepy eyes and four very scary claws. Its legs are odd and it is very unusual for an animal to have only three legs. Altogether it looks rather weird and unbelievable.

This is a wonderful car which looks a little funny, because it only has three wheels, but it has an incredible shape. The front of the car looks fantastic and it is a great colour – I love turquoise. It's an amazing car which can go very fast.

ADJECTIVES

Words to describe things that frighten you	Words to describe things that are unusual	Words to describe things that are good
creepy		

Do you know any other words that can go in this word map?

2 Complete these sentences with a suitable word from exercise 1.

a I've just seen a ......funny...... movie. It's a comedy and I laughed a lot.
b That woman is very .... She wears strange clothes and reads poetry on the bus.
c What a .... sports car. Does it go very fast?
d I don't like to be at home alone at night. I find it ....
e They say there are ghosts in that house. It's a .... place.
f This shop only sells dolls and gardening tools. What a .... shop!
g My grandfather likes to eat banana sandwiches. He's a little ....
h Did you see that .... bird? It only has one leg and one eye.
i What a .... digital camera! The pictures are so clear.

3 Which of the words in blue in exercise 1 could you use to describe these things?

a a creature with four hands ....strange............
b a person who never talks to other people ....
c a machine to travel in time ....
d a cemetery (where dead people are buried) ....
e a house that nobody has lived in for 20 years ....
f a space ship ....
g a car ....
h a movie poster for a horror film ....

4 Write suitable words to describe the pictures.

....
b ....
c ....
d ....

5 Write a description of one of the pictures using at least five adjectives.

....
....
....
....
....

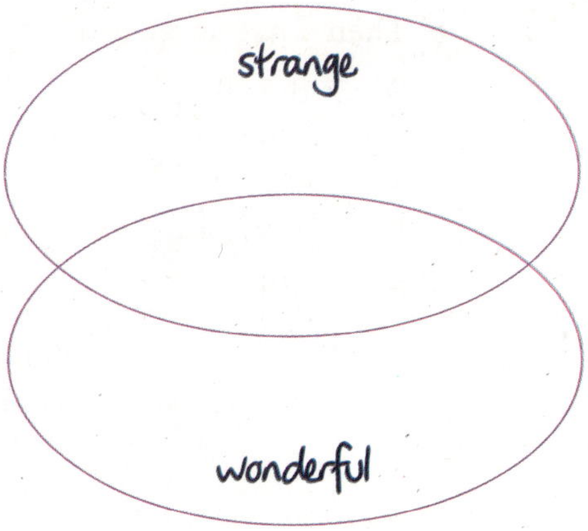

WORD BANK

Make a diagram like this in your Word Bank notebook with all the words you know for things that are strange, wonderful or both.

B Functions

Paying attention

1 Look at these pictures carefully. Then listen to Track 48 and write the numbers *1–6* in the boxes.

2 Listen to Track 48 again. Tick the words and expressions you hear.

a Yeah? ☐
b What happened next? ☐
c Really? ☐
d Uh-huh. ☐
e Then what happened? ☐
f What did she say? ☐
g What? ☐
h How weird! ☐
i That's funny. ☐
j Right. ☐
k That's impossible! ☐
l Wow! ☐
m And? ☐
n That's weird. ☐
o That's strange. ☐
p I see. ☐

3 Complete the chart with words and expressions from exercise 2.
Write *a–p*.

Things to show the speaker that you are paying attention	d
Asking questions	
Reacting to what the speaker says	

4 Complete this dialogue with expressions from the box.

Yeah?	What happened next?
Really?	~~Uh-huh.~~ Uh-huh.
Then what happened?	
What did she say?	What?
What?	How weird!
That's funny.	Right.
That's impossible!	Wow!
And?	That's weird.
That's strange.	I see.

JANE: So, let me tell you about what happened at the airport.
ROBBIE: (a) Uh-huh.
JANE: Well, I arrived early to check in.
ROBBIE: (b) ....
JANE: And then I went to get something to eat.
ROBBIE: (c) ....
JANE: While I was eating a sandwich I heard someone scream!
ROBBIE: (d) ....
JANE: Well, I ran to where I heard the scream.
ROBBIE: (e) ....
JANE: And, you'll never guess what!
ROBBIE: (f) ....
JANE: There was nobody there.
ROBBIE: (g) ....
JANE: Well, I looked and looked everywhere for the person in trouble.
ROBBIE: (h) ....
JANE: I never found anything. And do you know what was the worst thing?
ROBBIE: (i) ....
JANE: I missed the plane, because I was looking for the person who screamed.
ROBBIE: (j) ....

Now listen to Track 49 and compare your answers.

5 Listen to the story on Track 50 and reply as Robbie.

AUDIOSCRIPTS

Track 1

SONIA: So which is better, then, Fran, Marbella or Dublin?

FRAN: Marbella, definitely. It's more relaxing, and it's cheaper! And it's got lovely beaches.

SONIA: But we always go to the beach. I'd rather do something different this year. Something more interesting. Like a city. Like Dublin.

FRAN: There's a problem, then, Sonia.

SONIA: Oh? What's that?

FRAN: Because I like beaches. Well, I like beaches better than cities, anyway. And Marbella is sunnier too. And it always rains in Ireland, you know, Sonia.

SONIA: No, it doesn't. And anyway, rain or no rain, there's more to do in Dublin.

FRAN: Like what? Museums and things like that? I'd rather stay here in London!

SONIA: OK then. You go to the beach and I'll go to Dublin. How's that?

FRAN: Oh, all right. You win. This time. But no museums and no walking around in the rain!

Track 2

SAM: Which package is better, then?

JACK: Oh, Package 3, definitely. It's cheaper! Which do you prefer?

SAM: Me? I prefer Package 1. It sounds much nicer.

JACK: But it's more expensive and shorter. Anyway, I prefer summer holidays to winter holidays.

SAM: But the summer is nice here, too. I'd rather go in December, when it's dark and cold here.

JACK: OK, you win. But that's the only holiday we can take in the whole year then. Would you rather have just one holiday, or two? Think about it.

SAM: Oh. Maybe July is not so bad after all ...

Track 3

LISA: What's up, Maggie?

MAGGIE: Uh? Oh, I need to relax. Got any ideas?

LISA: Yes. Try exercise.

MAGGIE: Exercise?

LISA: Yeah. Go to a gym or something.

MAGGIE: No thanks. I don't like exercise.

LISA: OK, then. How about aromatherapy?

MAGGIE: What's that exactly?

LISA: It's a mixture of oils and smells and massage. Very, very relaxing.

MAGGIE: Massage? That's not for me, I'm afraid.

LISA: You ARE difficult Maggie.

MAGGIE: Sorry!

LISA: I know. You can close your eyes and count sheep. Slowly.

MAGGIE: How many sheep?

LISA: You could count up to, say, 33,781.

MAGGIE: Thirty three thousand, seven hundred ...

LISA: Maggie? Maggie ... ha ha.

Track 4

ROB: Hi Leyla! You don't look too happy. Problems?

LEYLA: I have exams next week and I don't know anything! What can I do to pass?

BEEP

LEYLA: Yeah, I looked at them but it doesn't help.

BEEP

LEYLA: Hmm, yes. But what about maths? I don't understand anything! Got any ideas?

BEEP

LEYLA: You're right. Let's forget about exams. Do you want to listen to my new J-Lo record?

Track 5

TV ANNOUNCER: Next on 5 it's *Soap Time* with *The Rich Cry Too.*

JANE: Do you want to go out for a pizza?

LISA: What, now? I can't. *The Rich Cry Too* is about to begin. Don't you watch it?

JANE: I hate soaps. They're silly stories.

LISA: Well, I don't agree. I think they're really exciting. They're my favourite programmes!

JANE: You're joking! Soap operas are for people who have nothing better to do.

LISA: No they're not. Oh, Shhhhh. It's about to start.

WOMAN 1: Danny was on the ground, bleeding and I ...

WOMAN 2: But you weren't to blame ...

WOMAN 1: No, but ... well, yes ... but now I'm going to take this back to him ...

JANE: Wow! Oh no! What's she doing? Actually, this is exciting!

LISA: Hmmm. What do you think of soaps now, eh?

Track 6

a

Well, what did you think about the film?

Terrific! Really fantastic.

b
What do you think of news programmes?
I think they're terrible. They're really boring.

c
What did you think of the new CD?
It's great! The Scissor Sisters are like – well, they're great!

d
Isn't this video great?
Do you really think so? I think it's awful.

Track 7

LOUISE: What do you think of documentaries?
DAMIAN: I think they're boring.
LOUISE: Do you really think so?
DAMIAN: Yes, don't you?
LOUISE: No. I think they're interesting. Well, sometimes.
DAMIAN: I think you're right. Only sometimes. I hate documentaries about animals, for example.
LOUISE: Oops! I bought you a DVD about birds for your birthday.
DAMIAN: You're joking!
LOUISE: No. I really did.
DAMIAN: Oh, well, birds are fine. Birds are good. Actually, I love birds!

Track 8

FRED: What are you doing, Bella?
BELLA: Looking for a job.
FRED: Any luck?
BELLA: Nah, there is nothing I fancy.
FRED: There must be something. Let's have a look ... This sounds fun. They're looking for someone to help out at the Animal Shelter.
BELLA: That's not for me. I'm not keen on animals.
FRED: Aren't you? I love animals. Anyway, how about this? They're looking for someone at the hamburger place.
BELLA: I can't stand fast food places. Can you imagine making hamburgers all day? What a horrible job!
FRED: All right then, how about babysitting. Here's someone looking for a babysitter.
BELLA: Well, I don't mind children. But look at the money. It's peanuts!
FRED: It's not that bad. Do you know, I like children, too. I'm pretty good with them. I think I'll call this person.
BELLA: Hey, that's not fair! I see the ad and you take the job.
FRED: Nothing's fair, Bella!

Track 9

MAX: I am thinking of teaching after college. But I'm not sure.
MOLLY: Teaching? You? But you don't like children.
MAX: I'm not very keen on them. But I don't hate them. Actually, I don't really mind children – for a short time!
MOLLY: I love little children but I can't stand big groups. I fancy a job teaching small groups.
MAX: Oh no, that's not for me. I want to get a temporary job to see if I like it.
MOLLY: That's a good idea.

Track 10

INTERVIEWER: How do you feel about children?
BEEP
INTERVIEWER: Right. Now, tell me two things you like about teaching.
BEEP
INTERVIEWER: And two things you definitely don't like?
BEEP
INTERVIEWER: So, do you think teaching is right for you?
BEEP

Track 11

KIM: What time shall we meet, Max?
MAX: I could be there by about 11.
KIM: OK, where do you suggest?
MAX: Well, Kim, I could wait at the top of the escalator, you know, by the entrance.
KIM: I've got a better idea. How about under the clock by platform 3?
MAX: OK. That sounds good. Eleven o'clock it is then. Under the clock.
KIM: Fine. See you there.

Track 12

JACKIE: Where's the best place to meet?
SANDY: Where do you suggest?
JACKIE: Why don't we meet at Café Commons?
SANDY: OK. What time?
JACKIE: Hmm. How about 7.30?
SANDY: That sounds great.
JACKIE: OK. 7.30 it is, then.
SANDY: See you there.

Track 13

BEEP
MAYA: Let's say 6 o'clock.
BEEP
MAYA: We could meet at the bus stop.
BEEP
MAYA: OK. Good idea. We'll meet at the restaurant.

BEEP

MAYA: See you there.

Track 14

a What's your name?
b When were you born?
c Are you married?
d Are your grandparents still living?
e Are you keen on anyone in particular?
f At what age did you start school?

Track 15

ANNE: I remember something that happened at school once. I got into a lot of trouble – and so did my friend Lucy. We had a history exam the next day, so we stayed up all night to study. We wanted to get good grades. Well, we wanted to pass anyway.

NINA: That sounds familiar.

ANNE: Anyway, so we talked, watched a video, had a good time. But we didn't study. Of course, in the morning, we were really worried. We didn't know any history! We were going to fail the exam.

NINA: I know the feeling. So what did you do?

ANNE: Well, we decided not to go to the exam and to make up an excuse for the teacher.

NINA: Uh, oh.

ANNE: Wait, I spoke to the teacher, looking really sad and told him: 'Oh, I'm really sorry, sir. But I couldn't come to the exam because, sadly, my grandmother died.'

NINA: Did he believe you?

ANNE: Yes, he did! He was very sympathetic, really nice. So I thought 'phew'! But then, Lucy came in, crying, and said 'I'm sorry I missed my exam. My grandmother died!' And he said 'Your grandmother died too!' And then he realised!

NINA: Oh, no! Didn't you plan your stories beforehand?

ANNE: No, we never thought of that!

NINA: How stupid! So, what happened then?

ANNE: Well, of course, the school phoned my parents, I was grounded for months. I had to go straight back home when school finished. But my grandmother thought it was all pretty funny.

Track 16

ALEX: I did something really stupid.

BERNIE: Let me guess! You lost your mobile phone again, right?

ALEX: No, no. I'm seeing Paula tonight, right? So I bought her some flowers.

BERNIE: That's nice.

ALEX: Yeah. But I put the flowers on the roof of the car, you know, to open the door.

BERNIE: Uh, oh.

ALEX: And I drove away with the flowers on the roof. Now I feel really stupid.

BERNIE: I know the feeling. So, buy her more flowers.

ALEX: I don't have money for the cinema <u>and</u> more flowers.

BERNIE: That sounds familiar!

Track 17

ALEX: I did something really stupid.

BEEP

ALEX: No, no. I'm seeing Paula tonight, right? So I bought her some flowers.

BEEP

ALEX: Yeah. But I put the flowers on the roof of the car, you know, to open the door.

BEEP

ALEX: And I drove away with the flowers on the roof. Now I feel really stupid.

BEEP

ALEX: I don't have money for the cinema <u>and</u> more flowers.

BEEP

Track 18

GIRL 1: I did something really stupid.

GIRL 2: Let me guess! You lost your glasses again.

GIRL 1: No. I bought a cake for my sister's birthday.

GIRL 2: That's kind.

GIRL 1: But I put it on my chair and I sat on it!

GIRL 2: How stupid! Buy her another cake!

GIRL 1: I haven't got any more money!

GIRL 2: I know the feeling!

Track 19

MATT: Hi Liz.

LIZ: Hi Matt.

MATT: Would you like to come rowing?

LIZ: Rowing?

MATT: Yeah. Rowing. You know. In a boat.

LIZ: Of course I know 'in a boat'. It's just that, well, you have a broken arm.

MATT: You're right! That's why I thought you could do the actual rowing.

LIZ: Oh no.

MATT: No? Why not?

LIZ: I'm not crazy about rowing, actually. I'm not very good at it.

MATT: Oh, right. Well, how about a walk?

LIZ: I'm a bit tired.

MATT: Or a coffee?

LIZ: Now you're talking!

Track 20

JAMIE: Hey, Nat. Would you like to come bowling?
NAT: Bowling? I'd love to, Jamie, but I can't. I have to work.
JAMIE: Oh well. Perhaps another day?
NAT: Yeah. Perhaps.

SUE: Hi, Sam. Do you fancy going to the cinema?
SAM: Hmm. I'm not sure, Sue. I went to the cinema on Saturday.
SUE: How about a pizza then?
SAM: That would be great. I'm really hungry.

TRICIA: Would you like to come to dinner tonight, Mike?
MIKE: I'd rather not, Tricia. I have to get up early tomorrow.
TRICIA: How about Friday then?
MIKE: I'm not really sure. Call me tomorrow, OK?
TRICIA: OK.

Track 21

BEEP
MIKE: A dance? Well, I don't really like dancing.
BEEP
MIKE: I'd love to, but I'm busy on Tuesday.
BEEP
MIKE: Now you're talking! Everybody says you're a great cook!

Track 22

1
WILLIAM: Did you bring that book I lent you, Katie?
KATIE: Oh, the book! I'm sorry, William. I forgot!
WILLIAM: Don't worry about it. You can give it to me tomorrow.
2
MAN 1: Watch out! You're spilling your drink on my foot!
MAN 2: Oops! Sorry!
MAN 1: That's OK. Just be a bit more careful.
3
TEACHER: Good morning, Johnson. Good of you to join us.
JOHNSON: I'm sorry Mrs Gordon!
TEACHER: Well, that's the third time this week, you know?
JOHNSON: I apologise. It won't happen again.
TEACHER: Apology accepted. Now, please can I have your essay?
JOHNSON: Essay?... er ... Oh, the essay. Sorry, I ... um ...
4
SHARON: Mum! I waited for hours in the rain and you never turned up!
MUM: I'm really sorry you waited so long, Sharon.
SHARON: Well it wasn't much fun. Why didn't you ring?
MUM: I tried to ring but your mobile was busy. You see, the car broke down. It wasn't much fun for me either!
SHARON: I'm sorry, mum. I didn't mean to upset you.
MUM: I'm not upset.

Track 23

a
MAN: You're late!
WOMAN: Sorry!
MAN: Well, we said 8 o'clock and it's 8.45 now.
WOMAN: I know. I'm sorry you waited so long.
MAN: It wasn't much fun, you know?
WOMAN: I said I'm sorry. I lost my laptop. That's why I'm late.
MAN: Oh, I'm really sorry. I didn't mean to upset you. Listen, do you still want to see the film?
b
WOMAN: Good afternoon, Mr Rice. I apologise for being late.
MAN: Yes, I see your appointment was at four.
WOMAN: I'm sorry. There was a lot of traffic.
MAN: Well, never mind. Now, open wide please.
WOMAN: Ouch!
MAN: Oops, sorry. Did that hurt?

Track 24

MAN: You're late!
BEEP
MAN: Well, we said 8 o'clock and it's 8.45 now.
BEEP
MAN: It wasn't much fun, you know?
BEEP
MAN: Oh, I'm really sorry. I didn't mean to upset you. Listen, do you still want to see the film?

Track 25

a
SUE: Hello.
HARRY: Hi Sue. It's Harry. Is Milly there?
SUE: No, she's out. Do you want me to say you called?
HARRY: No, that's OK. I'll call her later.
SUE: OK. See you.
HARRY: Bye.

b
OPERATOR: Hello, Language Centre. Can I help you?
HARRY: Could you put me through to Mr Rose?

OPERATOR: I'm sorry. The line is busy. Would you like to hold?
HARRY: Yes. I'll hold.
OPERATOR: Sorry to keep you waiting. The line is still engaged. Can I take a message?
HARRY: Yes. Could you tell Mr Rose that Harry Parker called? It's about his DVD player.
OPERATOR: Of course.

Track 26

1

SHOP: Hello. Best Electronics. Can I help you?
YOU: Could you put me through to the manager?
SHOP: Who's calling please?
YOU: This is Marcial López.
SHOP: Sorry, his line's engaged.
YOU: Could you take a message, please?
SHOP: Sure.
YOU: Please tell him that I bought an MP3 player at your shop. It doesn't work and I want my money back. Can you ask him to phone me on 34 56 07 48?

2

STEVE'S SISTER: Hello?
CHRIS: Hi, it's Chris. Is Steve there?
STEVE'S SISTER: No. He's out. Do you want him to phone you back?
CHRIS: Can you tell him I want the game I lent him back?
STEVE'S SISTER: Oh, here he is. You can tell him yourself.
CHRIS: Hi Steve. It's Chris. Listen, can I have my game back?

Track 27

BEEP
FRANCES: Hi. This is Frances. Can I speak to Carmen, please?
BEEP
FRANCES: When will she be back?
BEEP
FRANCES: Yes, please. Tell her Frances called. Can she meet me outside the cinema at 8.30, not at 8. I can't be there earlier.
BEEP
FRANCES: That's right. Who's speaking please?
BEEP
FRANCES: OK. Thanks for your help. Bye.

Track 28

JANE: I just want to say thank you.
CARL: You're welcome.
JANE: No really. You saved my life.
CARL: It was nothing.
JANE: No really. Thanks to you it was a great success.
CARL: Well, that's a relief.
JANE: Seriously, thank you for everything.
CARL: Sure.

Track 29

1

YOUNG MAN: It's just what I wanted.
GRANDMA: I'm glad you like it.

2

YOUNG MAN: Thank you for all your help.
YOUNG WOMAN: You're welcome.

3

WOMAN: Thanks to you the party was a great success.
OLD WOMAN: It was a pleasure.

4

YOUNG WOMAN: Thanks so much for helping me with my homework.
OLDER MAN: No problem.

5

WOMAN: Thanks a lot for dinner.
MAN: Don't mention it.

Track 30

a

BEEP
YOUR FRIEND: You're welcome.

b

YOUR FRIEND: Thanks so much for the great DVD. I love it.
BEEP

c

BEEP
YOUR BROTHER: No problem.

d

BEEP
YOUR MOTHER: I'm so glad you liked it.

Track 31

a It was awful. So boring. It was slow and really romantic and I didn't find it enjoyable at all.
b Wow! What a great movie – it had lots of action and I found it so enjoyable. It was really good fun watching the cars racing through the streets of a large city.
c It was so scary! I had to close my eyes most of the time. There were these people killing other people – it was so violent.
d I loved it! It was so funny – I laughed from beginning to end. These movies are so enjoyable. I wish there were more movies like this one.

Track 32

a Have you seen *Days of Laughter*?
BEEP

b Have you seen *Night of the Zombie Killers*?
BEEP
c Have you seen *The Long Hot Summer*?
BEEP
d Have you seen *The New York Race*?
BEEP

Track 33

WOMAN: Arts Cinema. Can I help you?
MAN: Yes please. I'd like some tickets for *The Cuba File*, please. For today.
WOMAN: OK. What time do you want to see the film?
MAN: 6.20.
WOMAN: And how many tickets would you like?
MAN: Two, please.
WOMAN: Where would you like to sit?
MAN: Could we have an aisle seat at the back?
WOMAN: Yes, I think I can do that. Can you give me your credit card number?
MAN: Sure. It's 4552 …
WOMAN: OK sir, the payment's gone through. Come along 15 minutes before the performance starts and your tickets will be here.
MAN: Great.
WOMAN: Is there anything else I can do for you.
MAN: No thanks, that's all. Goodbye.

Track 34

MAN: Murray's Restaurant here.
WOMAN: Hello. I'd like to book a table, please.
MAN: Certainly. What day is that for?
WOMAN: Next Wednesday, please.
MAN: Sure. And how many people is that for?
WOMAN: Just for two.
MAN: Two people on Wednesday. OK, and what time were you thinking of?
WOMAN: 8 o'clock.
MAN: 8 p.m. Right. And what's your name?
WOMAN: Jennifer Healey.
MAN: OK, Ms Healey. Next Wednesday at 8 o'clock, table for two.
WOMAN: Thank you very much.

RECEPTIONIST: The Garden Hotel. Can I help you?
MAN: Yes, I'd like a room for two nights, please.
RECEPTIONIST: Two nights? Is that for tonight?
MAN: Yes, tonight and tomorrow night.
RECEPTIONIST: I'm afraid the hotel is full tonight.
MAN: Oh dear. What about tomorrow?
RECEPTIONIST: We have one room available tomorrow.
MAN: OK, can I book that room, please?
RECEPTIONIST: Certainly sir. Can I have your credit card number?
MAN: Yes. It's 6475 7564 …

Track 35

MAN: Murray's Restaurant here.
BEEP
MAN: Certainly. What day is that for?
BEEP
MAN: Sure. And how many people is that for?
BEEP
MAN: OK, and what time were you thinking of?
BEEP
MAN: Right. And what's your name?
BEEP
MAN: OK. Your table is booked.
BEEP

RECEPTIONIST: The Garden Hotel. Can I help you?
BEEP
RECEPTIONIST: Is that for tonight?
BEEP
RECEPTIONIST: I'm afraid the hotel is full tonight.
BEEP
RECEPTIONIST: We have one room available tomorrow.
BEEP
RECEPTIONIST: Certainly sir. Can I have your credit card number?
BEEP

Track 36

a
Why don't you let me carry your bags?
They are very heavy. Thanks.

b
I don't think I can reach the button.
Allow me. I'll press it for you.

c
Would you like some help with your homework?
No, thanks. I can do it by myself.

d
Can I help you to finish those forms?
Thanks. I need to get home early tonight.

e
Shall I make you something to eat?
Don't worry about it. I'm fine. I ate about an hour ago.

Track 37

Conversation a

WOMAN: Would you like me to help you with dinner?
MAN: Thanks. That would be great. Can you chop those onions?

Conversation b

YOUNG MAN: You look tired. How about if I make you a nice cup of tea?

OLD LADY: Thanks, dear, but I'm fine. I'll have some tea later.

Conversation c

OLD MAN: I can't open this door.

YOUNG MAN: Allow me. It is very heavy.

Conversation d

YOUNG WOMAN: Why don't you do the first part of the reading and I'll do the second part, so we save time?

YOUNG MAN: Sure. It's about 100 pages altogether.

Conversation e

YOUNG WOMAN: Can I help you to do the shopping?

OLD WOMAN: Don't worry about it. I only need to get a few things.

Track 38

a DAD: Would you like me to help you, son?

BEEP

DAD: Oh, OK.

b YOUNG MAN: Wow! What a mess! How about if we help you to get the room ready?

BEEP

YOUNG MAN: Right. OK.

Track 39

RACHEL: What are you going to do when you leave school?

JAKE: I'm going to study criminology at university.

RACHEL: Criminology? What's that?

JAKE: Oh, it's the study of all things connected with crime and criminals.

RACHEL: Oh, that sounds interesting. So are you going to be someone who goes to court? What do you call it?

JAKE: A barrister?

RACHEL: Oh yes, that's it. A barrister.

JAKE: No, I'm not going to be a barrister. I'm going to be a criminology teacher. What about you? What are you going to study?

RACHEL: I'm not sure yet.

Track 40

KRISTINA: Ellie, what does 'talent' mean?

ELLIE: Oh, it means something that you are good at.

KRISTINA: OK, I understand. Like I have a talent for singing?

ELLIE: That's right.

KRISTINA: And what do you call it when you like doing something, even if you are not good at it?

ELLIE: You mean, like a hobby?

KRISTINA: Yes, a hobby.

ELLIE: Usually people who have hobbies have some kind of ability for the thing they like to do, but not always.

KRISTINA: What do you mean by 'ability'?

ELLIE: Ability means being able to do something, like an activity.

KRISTINA: Activity? What's that?

ELLIE: An activity is something you do.

KRISTINA: Wow! I need a dictionary. Then I could find these words for myself. How do you say 'find out something for yourself'?

ELLIE: Discover. Yes, I think you need a dictionary, Kristina.

Track 41

ABBY: I really don't like parties.

BEEP

CHRIS: Shy? Are you shy?

BEEP

CHRIS: You mean, it frightens you.

BEEP

CHRIS: That's strange, because you're very popular.

BEEP

CHRIS: It's when a lot of people like you.

BEEP

CHRIS: Oh, you mean when people pay you a lot of attention.

BEEP

Track 42

ANNE: Can I ask you something?

CATH: Sure.

ANNE: What's the best film you've ever seen?

CATH: That's difficult.

ANNE: Sorry.

CATH: No, that's all right. The best film? I think it's *The Usual Suspects*. I saw it on TV last week. What about you?

ANNE: That's easy. *Jaws*. You know, the one with the great white shark.

CATH: Yes, I liked that too.

ANNE: I've seen it about 15 times!

Track 43

JAYNE: What's the most delicious meal you've ever eaten?

DAVID: I'll have to think.

JAYNE: Take your time.

DAVID: It was the meal my mum cooked for my 18th birthday.

JAYNE: What did she cook?

DAVID: She made roast chicken with roast potatoes and gravy.

JAYNE: That sounds nice.

DAVID: Yes, everyone loved it!

Track 44

WOMAN: What was the most delicious meal you've ever eaten?

BEEP

MAN: Who cooked it?

BEEP

MAN: What did that person 'or people' cook?

BEEP

Track 45

CHARLES: I've just started going to a new gym.

MARTINA: Oh, really? Me too. Which gym?

CHARLES: It's called 'Get Fit'.

MARTINA: That's my gym too. I love it.

CHARLES: So do I. But I don't like the trainer.

MARTINA: Neither do I. He's unfriendly, but I feel great.

CHARLES: I don't. I've only been twice.

MARTINA: So have I. I just don't have the time.

CHARLES: Neither do I. I'm really busy at work.

MARTINA: So am I. I can't go to the gym today.

CHARLES: I can't go either. I have to work late.

MARTINA: I need more time off. I have to talk to my boss.

CHARLES: So do I! If we want to get healthy, we'll need to go to the gym more than once a week!

Track 46

RICHARD: I need to wear glasses.

ALICE: So do I. I can't read the newspaper very well.

RICHARD: Neither can I. It gives me a headache.

ALICE: Me too! But I don't know any good opticians.

RICHARD: Neither do I, but my sister knows one.

ALICE: That's good. Can you give me the name when you've asked her?

RICHARD: Sure. I need to have my eyes tested soon.

ALICE: I do, too. Call me tonight, I'm not going out.

RICHARD: I'm not either. I'll call you around seven.

ALICE: OK. Thanks.

Track 47

MARIA: Hi, my name's Maria Smith.

BEEP

MARIA: Oh really? Where are you from?

BEEP

MARIA: Me too! Where do you live?

BEEP

MARIA: So do I. Are you married?

BEEP

MARIA: Neither am I. What do you do?

BEEP

MARIA: I'm a student, too. What are you studying?

BEEP

MARIA: No, I'm not. I'm studying psychology.

Track 48

JACKIE: Remember I told you that something strange once happened to me?

RONNIE: Yes, I remember. What is it?

JACKIE: Well ... It happened about two years ago. I went out for the night and I got home late.

RONNIE: Uh-huh.

JACKIE: Well, as I was going up the stairs I heard our dog, Rex, barking.

RONNIE: Yeah?

JACKIE: I was surprised because he'd been really sick.

RONNIE: That's strange.

JACKIE: So, anyway, I went to bed and in the night I heard him in my room.

RONNIE: And how did he seem?

JACKIE: He seemed fine, just like his old self, so I felt really happy.

RONNIE: So what happened then?

JACKIE: Well, I woke up in the morning and I looked out of the window, and I saw him playing and then he disappeared into some bushes.

RONNIE: Then what happened?

JACKIE: So then I went downstairs and gave him some food because his bowl was empty.

RONNIE: Right.

JACKIE: Just as I was having breakfast the phone rang and it was my mother. 'Where are you?', I said. 'Rex is much better now, but when I got up there was no food in his bowl.' And, you'll never guess what she said ...

RONNIE: What? What did she say?

JACKIE: She said, 'What are you talking about? We're at the vet's surgery and Rex has just died.'

RONNIE: That's impossible!

JACKIE: So I argued with her and then ran to find Rex.

RONNIE: And?

JACKIE: He was gone. The house was empty and he wasn't outside either.

RONNIE: Wow! That's weird.

Track 49

JANE: So, let me tell you about what happened at the airport.

ROBBIE: Uh-huh.

JANE: Well, I arrived early to check in.

ROBBIE: Right.

JANE: And then I went to get something to eat.

ROBBIE: Uh-huh.

JANE: While I was eating a sandwich I heard someone scream!

ROBBIE: Then what happened?
JANE: Well, I ran to where I heard the scream.
ROBBIE: Yeah?
JANE: And, you'll never guess what?
ROBBIE: What?
JANE: There was nobody there.
ROBBIE: That's weird! What happened next?
JANE: Well, I looked and looked everywhere for the person in trouble.
ROBBIE: And?
JANE: I never found anything. And do you know what was the worst thing?
ROBBIE: What?
JANE: I missed the plane, because I was looking for the person who screamed.
ROBBIE: Wow!

Track 50

JANE: So, let me tell you about what happened at the airport.
BEEP
JANE: Well, I arrived early to check in.
BEEP
JANE: And then I went to get something to eat.
BEEP
JANE: While I was eating a sandwich I heard someone scream!
BEEP
JANE: Well, I ran to where I heard the scream.
BEEP
JANE: And, you'll never guess what!
BEEP
JANE: There was nobody there.
BEEP
JANE: Well, I looked and looked everywhere for the person in trouble.
BEEP
JANE: I never found anything. And do you know what was the worst thing?
BEEP
JANE: I missed the plane, because I was looking for the person who screamed.
BEEP

Answer key

Unit 1

Vocabulary

1 a post office b car hire c cash dispenser
d police station e travel agent f petrol staion
g shopping centre h bus stop
2 a phone box b car park c road signs
d tea bag e traffic lights f letter box
g underground station h cricket match
3 a a phrase book b a hotel room c a sun hat
d sun glasses e a pocket calculator
f a sleeping bag g a guide book
h a video camera
4 a a book shop b a chicken sandwich
c a music shop d a fruit cake
e a chocolate biscuit f a tea cup g an armchair
h a newspaper i a car park j a concert ticket

Functions

Background information

Marbella is a seaside town on the south coast of Spain. It is a very popular destination for Europeans seeking sunshine and beaches. Dublin is the capital of the Irish Republic. It is a cosmopolitan city and it has many museums, galleries and other places of interest.

2 Sample answers:
Fran, Picture A: she likes lying on the beach.
Sonia: Picture B: she likes sightseeing and learning about different cultures.
3 a relaxing b cheaper c interesting d sunnier
4 a Dublin
b You win.
5 Asking about preferences:
So which is better, then?
What's that?
Expressing preferences:
..... definitely.
I'd rather ....
I like ....
I like .... better than ....
6 a Which do you prefer? b I prefer
c I'd rather d Would you rather

Unit 2

Vocabulary

1 *Sample answers*
a a bowl of soup
b a slice of bread
c a cup of tea
d a drop of lemon juice
e a jug of orange juice
f a pinch of salt
g a spoonful of sugar
h a glass of milk
2 a piece – of furniture, of homework, of advice, of information, of clothing, of news.
3 a pieces of homework b piece of news
c piece of furniture d piece of advice
e piece of information f piece of clothing
4 a a bowl of soup
b a cup of tea
c a drop of lemon juice
d a slice of bread
e a glass of orange juice
f a bowl of ice cream
g a tablespoon of cream

Functions

1 a, e, d, b, c
2 a gym b oils c massage d eyes e sheep f sheep
3 Got any ideas? How about...? You can...
You could ... Try ...
4 a Try having a cup of warm milk before bed.
b How about not eating too much at night?
c Try not to watch television in bed.
d You could listen to some relaxing music.
e How about having a long warm bath?
f You can go for a short walk.
5 a Try studying your notes.
b You can/could do some of the practice questions, too.
c You can/could do some of the exercises in the book.
6 a What can I do
b Try
c can do
d Got any
e could

Unit 3

Vocabulary

1 a read a comic/a magazine/a newspaper/a report/the weather forecast (in the paper)
b watch a programme/the news/a report/the weather forecast (on television)
c listen to a programme/the news/a report/the weather forecast (on the radio)
2 documentary e
soap opera a
cartoon h
game show c
news b
reality show d
sitcom (short for situational comedy) g
talk show f

3 Radio: programme, station, presenter, newsreader, disc jockey (DJ)
Television: programme, channel, presenter, reporter, news reader, disc jockey (DJ), station
Newspapers and magazines: article, headline, journalist
4 *Sample answers*
a Well, you could read a newspaper, or listen to the news.
b Well, you could/can read a magazine.
c Well, you can/could watch television or read a comic.
d Well, you can/could watch a film or read a magazine/book.
e Well, you can/could listen to/watch the weather forecast.
f Well, you can/could watch television, or read a magazine or listen to the radio.
g Well, you can/could read an article.

Functions

1 They are talking about what to watch on TV. They don't agree.
2 a Lisa b Jane c Lisa d Lisa e Lisa f Jane g Jane h Jane
3 a 8 b 3 c 6 d 4 e 2 f 5 g 7 h 1
4 Asking for an opinion: What do you think of ...?
Giving an opinion: I hate soaps ... I think they're really exciting.
Agreeing: ... this is exciting!
Questioning an opinion: You're joking!
Disagreeing: No they're not. I don't agree.
5 Really good: great, terrific, (really) fantastic
Really bad: terrible, (really) boring, awful
6 a 2 b 5 c 4 d 1 e 3
7 a do you think of
b think so
c I think they're interesting
d I think you're right
e documentaries about animals

Unit 4

Vocabulary

1 a Job (countable) b work c job d job e jobs f job g work
2 a 1 b 4 c 5 d 3 e 6 f 2
3 a works with b work on c work for d work out e work as f working in
4 a job b work c work d job e job, work
5 a in, bouncer
b in, with, out, as, teacher
c for, on, out, as, disc jockey
d for, with, as, pest controller
e for, with, on, as, roadie

Functions

1 The ads the friends discuss are: Calling animal lovers, Burger Lads and Wanted (babysitting).
2 a Bella b Fred c Bella d Bella e Bella f Fred g Bella h Fred
3 **Ways to say you like something:**
I fancy ... (Be careful! When this is followed by a verb, it requires an -ing form.)
I like (children).
I don't mind (children).
I love (animals).
It's not that bad.
Ways to say you don't like something:
That's not for me.
I'm not keen on ... (animals).
I can't stand (fast food places). (Be careful! When this is followed by a verb, it requires an -ing form.)
4 a hate b dislike c not like d like e love
5 a don't like b keen on c hate
d don't (really) mind e love
f can't stand g fancy

Unit 5

Vocabulary

1 a Airport: Picture 4
b Bus (Coach) station: Picture 3
c Ferry terminal: Picture 1
d Railway (underground) station: Picture 2
2 At the airport: check-in desk, escalator, passport control gate, plane
In the bus station: bays, barrier
At the ferry terminal: barrier
In the railway station: ticket office, escalator, platform
3 a board b Take c Board d Go e leaves f Take g leaves h Go i arrives j Change k change l Check-in
4 a escalator
b platform
c ticket
d airport
e lift
f board
g gate
h barrier
i terminal
j station
5 a airport b check-in desk c ticket d escalator e terminal f gate g boarded h arrived i passport control j luggage k took l taxi

Functions

1 a there b where c wait
d by (near, at, next to) e about
f good (possible) g Under h there

2 Asking for suggestions: b, j, k.
Making suggestions: c, d, e, i, l.
Offering alternatives: g.
Agreeing: a, f, h.
3 a, h, d, f, c, g, e, b
4 *Sample answers*
a When shall we meet?
b Where is the best place to meet?
c I've got a better suggestion. Why don't we meet at the restaurant at 8?
d That sounds great. See you at 8, then.

Unit 6

Vocabulary

1 **a** birth, **b** childhood, **c** adolescence (teens), romance, **d** education, **e** adulthood, work, **f** marriage, **g** parenthood.
2 birth: to be born, to have a baby
education: to graduate from (university), to start school
work: to work as a (doctor, programmer, etc.), to get a job
romance: to fall in love (with somebody), to be keen on someone
marriage: to get married, to marry someone
death: to die, to be dead.
3 **a** had **b** started **c** was keen **d** graduated from **e** got **f** worked as **g** fell in love **h** married **i** got married **j** dead **k** died
4 **a** was born on
b started school, graduated from
c married, got married
d got a job, worked as
e is now dead, died

Functions

1 a
2, 3
Making comments: b, a
I know what you mean.
Exclamations: e, d, c
How funny!, Wow!, Really?, No!, You're joking!
4 **a** How funny!
b I know what you mean. I know the feeling. That sounds familiar.
c Oh, no! Uh, oh.
d Wow! Really? No! You're joking! Oh, no!
e How stupid!
5 **a** Let me guess! You lost your mobile again, right?
b That's nice.
c Uh, oh.
d I know the feeling. So, buy her more flowers.
e That sounds familiar!
7 **a** Let me guess! You lost your glasses again.
b That's kind.
c How stupid! Buy her another cake!
d I know the feeling!

Unit 7

Vocabulary

1 bowling, boxing, pool
2 **a** golf course **b** football pitch **c** baseball field **d** bowling alley
3 **a** golf course **b** boxing ring **c** baseball field **d** pool table **e** tennis court **f** football pitch **g** bowling alley
4 **a** bowling/sailing/skating
b swimming/shopping/cycling
c dancing/rowing/bowling
d baseball practice
e horses/motorcycles/a bicycle
f football/golf
5 **a** tennis court **b** football pitch **c** boxing ring **d** golf course **e** bowling alley **f** baseball field **g** pool tables

Functions

1 **a** to come **b** a boat **c** I know **d** broken arm **e** That's why **f** do **g** Why not **h** crazy about **i** very good
2 **a** Do you fancy going rowing?
b Do you want to go rowing?
c How about going rowing?
d Would you like to go rowing?
3 Saying yes: I'd love to. That would be great. What a fantastic idea! Why not? Yes, OK, Yes, please. Now you're talking!
Not sure: I'd love to, but... I'm not really sure. Perhaps.
Saying no: I'd rather not. No, thanks.
4, 5
a bowling (Would you like to come …), no (I'd love to but I can't.)
b 1 to the cinema (Do you fancy going …), not sure (I'm not sure.), 2 for a pizza (How about …), yes (That would be great.)
c 1 to dinner tonight (Would you like to come …), no (I'd rather not …), 2 to dinner on Friday (How about …), not sure (I'm not really sure.)

Unit 8

Vocabulary

1 **a** proud **b** nervous **c** happy **d** sad **e** excited **f** angry **g** frightened **h** in love **i** jealous
2 Positive feelings: to be/feel – happy, proud, excited, in love
Negative feelings: to be/feel – sad, angry, nervous, frightened, jealous
3 happiness – happy
sadness – sad
nervousness – nervous
excitement – excited
amusement – amused
disappointment – disappointed
anger – angry

pride – proud
jealousy – jealous
fright – frightened
Two common endings for these nouns: *+ness*, *+ment*

4 a sad b nervous c proud d happy
e excited/nervous f angry g jealous h excited

Functions

1 a Dialogue 2
b Dialogue 3
c Dialogue 4
d Dialogue 1

2 I apologise.
Sorry!
I'm sorry that you waited so long.
I didn't mean to upset you.
Apology accepted.
That's OK.
Don't worry about it.

3 1 Dialogue b
2 Dialogue a

4 a I'm sorry you waited so long.
b I said I'm sorry.
c I didn't mean to upset you.
d I apologise for being late.
e I'm sorry.
f sorry.

Unit 9

Vocabulary

1 a (socket) 4
b (headset) 5
c (power button) 3
d (plug) 1
e (volume control) 2
f (output) 6

2 The phrasal verb can appear at the start of the sentence, or the preposition can appear on its own at the end of the sentence.

3 Plug in: the TV, the computer, the headset, the light, the radio
switch on/off: the TV, the computer, the light, the radio
turn on/off: the TV, the computer, the light, the radio
turn up/down: the TV, the radio, the volume

4 a Turn down the volume.
b Turn up the volume.
c Turn on the radio/TV.
d Switch on the light.
e Turn down the volume.
f Plug in the TV.
g Switch on the power button.

5 a 7 b 3 c 1 d 5 e 6 f 4 g 2

6 a Put the headset on.
b Switch the light off when you go.
c Turn the volume up.
d Turn the TV on.
e Turn the computer off when you finish.
f Plug the printer in before you use it.
g Pick the phone up.

7 a turn up
b turn off
c turn on
d Put on
e plug in
f turn up

Functions

1 Dialogue a: 6, 2, 1, 4, 5, 3
Dialogue b: 1, 4, 5, 2, 3, 6, 7

2 Offering help:
Can I help you? Can I take a message? (Formal)
Do you want me to say you called? (Informal)
Making a request:
Could you tell Mr Rose that Harry Parker called? (Formal)
(Can you tell her to call me?) not in dialogues but an informal request to add to the chart if wanted
Asking to speak to someone:
Could you put me through to Mr Rose? (Formal)
Is Milly there? (Informal)

3 *Sample answers*
Could you put me through to the manager, please?
This is ....
Could you take a message, please?
Please tell him that ...

4 The manager.
Steve is out.

5 a Hello? Best Electronics.
Hello?
Hi. It's Chris.
b Could you put me through to the manager, please?
Can you ask him to phone me?
Is Steve there?
c Sorry, his line's engaged.
Sample answer
Who's calling?
Sorry, she's out.
I'm not sure, can I take a message?
Can she meet you outside the cinema at 8.30 not 8.00?
My name's ...

Unit 10

Vocabulary

1 a cash b credit card c receipt d to the shops
e cheque f gold watch g shop assistant
h wrapping up i unwrapping

2 a 12 b 10 c 11 d 8 e 6 f 1 g 5 h 3 i 7 j 2
k 4 l 9

3 a Lucy went to the shops.
b She was looking for something for her friend Peter.
c She chose a gold watch.
d, e She didn't pay by cheque/She didn't pay in cash.
f She paid by credit card.
g The shop assistant wrapped up the watch.

h She asked for a receipt.
i She gave the watch to Peter.
j Peter unwrapped the present.
k Later, Peter took the watch back to the shop.
l He changed it for something else.

4 a gave b change c change d change e receipt f receipt g receipt h change

Functions

1 d

2 a say thank you b welcome c saved my life d nothing e a great success f Well, that's g for everything

3 a It's just what I wanted. [2]
b It's really kind of you. [1, 2, 3]
c Many thanks for (the present/helping me doing the shopping). [1, 2 or 3]
d Thank you for all your help/everything you've done for me. [1 & 3]
e Thank you so much for ...ing. [1 & 3]
f Thanks a lot. [1, 2, 3]
g Thanks to you the ... was a great success. [3]
h You saved my life! Thanks. [3]

4 a It's just what I wanted. I'm glad you like it.
b Thank you for all your help. You're welcome.
c Thanks to you the party was a great success. It was a pleasure.
d Thanks so much for helping me with my homework. No problem.
e Thanks a lot for dinner. Don't mention it.

5 a 4 b 5 c 1 d 3 e 2

Unit 11

Vocabulary

1 Photograph b

2 a review
b curtain
c boring
d slow
e clapped
f performance
g stage
h booked
i moving

3 a review b book c stage d audience e curtain f play g clapped h performance

4 Conversation a: 3
Conversation b: 4
Conversation c: 1
Conversation d: 2

Functions

1 a What time do you want to see the film?
b how many tickets would you like?
c Where would you like to sit?
d Can you give me your credit card number?
e Is there anything else I can do for you?

2 Offering a service: Can I help you?
Saying what you want: **e** I'd like a room for two nights **f** I'd like to book a table.
Asking for details: **b** How many people is that for? **n** What dates are you thinking of? **o** When is that for?
Saying it's possible/not possible: **d** I think we can do that, **l** That's fine, **g** I'm afraid that that performance is sold out, **h** I'm afraid there aren't any tickets left for that performance, **i** I'm afraid we're full tomorrow, **j** I'm sorry sir. The hotel is full on March 19th.
Getting a credit card number: Can you give me your credit card number?.
Saying what the customer should do: Come along 15 minutes before the performance starts.
Ending the conversation: **m** We look forward to seeing you on Thursday.
Describing where: **a** at the front **c** in the middle somewhere **k** not too near the back.

3 Conversation 1
i, e, l, j, k, b, g, h, f, d, a, c
Conversation 2
h, i, d, g, j, a, f, e, b, c

Unit 12

Vocabulary

1

Verbs	Nouns
clone	clone
protect	protection
cook	cooking
move	movement
defend	defence
Nouns	**Adjectives**
employment	employed, unemployed
plant	planted
interest	interested
inspiration	inspired
destruction	destroyed

2 a movement b inspiration c cooking d plants e interests f employment g destroyed h move

3 a interested b move c protects d activist e speeches g inspiration h married

4

XXXX	scientistscience	scientific
discover	discovery	discovered
interest	interest	interested (in)
destroy	destruction	destroyed
XXXX	environment/ environmentalist	environmental
plant	plant	planted
protect	protection	protected
marry	marriage	married
move	movement	moved/moving
act/activate	activist	active

5 a science, environmentalist b environmental c destruction, environment d plant e discovery f movements, protect g married, marriage

Functions

1 a 3 b 4 c 5 d 1 e2

2 a at the supermarket (mentions 'bags' and 'heavy')
b in a lift (mentions 'pressing the button')
c at school (mentions 'homework')
d at the office (mentions 'getting home early')
e at home (mentions 'making something to eat')

3 **Offering help:**
Why don't you let me ..?
Would you like some help ..?
Can I help you ...?
Shall I ...?
Allow me.
Accepting help:
Thanks.
Refusing help:
Don't worry about it.
I'm fine.
No, thanks.
I can do it by myself.

4 a Would you like, would be, Can you
b How about, Thanks
c Allow me
d Why don't, Sure
e Can I, Don't worry

Unit 13

Vocabulary

1 a Emily b Abigail c Barry d Matt e Marissa f Phil

2 a sporty b understanding c practical d sociable e confident f creative g artistic h logical

3 a 7 b 6 c 8 d 2 e 5 f 4 g 3 h 1

4 a green fingers
b practical
c artistic
d creative
e sociable
f sporty

Functions

1 i, e, g, c, f, h, a, d, b

2 a mean b means c call d mean e mean f What's g say

3 a do, mean
b that
c does, mean
d do you say
e do you call it

4 a 4 b 5 c 2 d 1 e 3

5 a What do you call it
b How do you call it
c What does that mean
d How do you say this

Unit 14

Vocabulary

1 a minute b tiny c small d big e large f enormous g huge h gigantic

2 a low – high, narrow – wide, short – tall
b tall, high
c high, low
d long, wide, narrow, deep, shallow
e long, wide, high, low

3 a large b enormous c minute d tiny e big f gigantic g small h huge

4 a minute b tiny c small d big e large f huge g enormous h gigantic

5 a shallow b wide c high d wide e tall f deep

Functions

1 a something b Sure c film d difficult e right f think g about h know i too

3 a What's the most beautiful thing you've ever seen?
b What's the most delicious food you've ever eaten/had?
c What's the most boring book you've ever read?
d What's the most frightening experience you've ever had?
e What's the best concert you've ever been to/seen?
f What's the worst food you've ever eaten/had?
g What's the ugliest thing you've ever seen?

4 a Take your time.
b That sounds nice.
c She made roast chicken with roast potatoes and gravy.
d I'll have to think.
e Yes, everyone loved it!
f What's the most delicious meal you've ever eaten?
g What did she cook?
h It was the meal my mum cooked for my 18th birthday.

5 f, d, a, h, g, c, b, e

Unit 15

Vocabulary

1 a forehead b brain c hair d chin e neck f lips g teeth h tongue i nostril j earlobe k eyebrow l eyeball m eyelashes

2 a mouth, lips, teeth (eyes)
b lips, tongue, teeth
c mouth, lips
d eyelashes, eye
e eyelid
f brain (senses)
g ears
h ears
i eyes, eyeballs
j nose, nostrils
k tongue

3 **a** eyebrow **b** lips **c** eyeball **d** hair **e** neck **f** tooth **g** mouth **h** brain **i** earlobe **j** tongue **k** nostril **l** eyelashes **m** forehead **n** chin

4 **a** teeth **b** earlobes **c** eyelashes **d** nostrils **e** chin **f** lips **g** hair **h** forehead **i** eyebrows **j** eyeballs **k** tongue **l** neck **m** brain

Functions

1 **a** too **b** too **c** So **d** Neither **e** So **f** Neither **g** So **h** either **i** So

2 **a** Both **b** Both **c** Both **d** M **e** Both **f** Both **g** Both **h** Both **i** Both

3 **Affirmative:**
I love my gym. So do I. I do, too. Me too. I'm very healthy. So am I. I am, too. Me too.
Negative:
I don't do much exercise. Neither do I. I don't, either.
I'm not very fit. Neither am I. I'm not either.

4 **a** So do I.
b Neither can I.
c Me too!
d Neither do I
e I do, too.
f I'm not either.

5 *Sample answers*
a So is Claire's. Claire's is, too.
b So is Maria. Maria is, too.
c So is Claire./Claire is, too.
d Maria isn't.
e Neither is Maria./Maria isn't, either.
f So does Claire./Claire does, too.

6 **a** too **b** Me too! **c** So do I. **d** not **e** Neither am **f** I'm a student, too **g** too **h** I'm not

Unit 16

Vocabulary

1 words to describe things that frighten you: creepy, scary, weird
words to describe things that are unusual: strange, fantastic, odd, unusual, weird, funny, unbelievable, incredible, amazing
words to describe things that are good: wonderful, incredible, fantastic, great, unbelievable, amazing

2 **a** funny, wonderful, incredible, fantastic, great, amazing
b strange, odd, unusual, funny
c wonderful, incredible, fantastic, great, amazing
d creepy, scary
e creepy, scary
f strange, odd, unusual, weird, funny
g strange, odd, unusual, weird, funny
h strange, odd, unusual, weird, funny
i wonderful, incredible, fantastic, great, amazing

3 **a** strange, weird, unbelievable, odd
b strange, odd, unusual, weird, funny
c wonderful, incredible, fantastic, great, amazing, strange, odd, unusual, weird, funny (depends on whether you think it is good or strange to travel in time)
d creepy, scary, frightening
e creepy, scary, frightening
f wonderful, incredible, fantastic, great, amazing
g wonderful, incredible, fantastic, great, terrific, amazing, strange, odd, unusual, weird, funny (depends on the car!)
h creepy, scary, frightening

Functions

1 **a** 2 **b** 6 **c** 5 **d** 1 **e** 4 **f** 3

2 Yeah? Uh-huh. Then what happened?
What did she say? What? Right. That's impossible!
Wow! And? That's weird. That's strange.

3 Things to show the speaker that you are paying attention: a, c, d, j, m, p
Asking questions: b, e, f
Reacting to what the speaker says: g, h, i, k, l, n, o

4 **a** Uh-huh.
b Right.
c Uh-huh.
d Then what happened?
e Yeah?
f What?
g That's weird. What happened next?
h And?
i What?
j Wow!